Knitted Gifts *for* All Seasons

Knitted Gifts

for
All Seasons

EASY PROJECTS TO MAKE AND SHARE

WENDY BERNARD

ABRAMS, NEW YORK

CONTENTS

INTRODUCTION

In my family, we had two knitting grandmas, and that meant we got to reap the rewards of both sets of hands and hearts. When I was really little and living in my hometown of Minneapolis, Minnesota, I remember placing wet hand-knit mittens on my paternal grandma Iva's radiator to dry after playing outside in the snow. Those were perfunctory mittens; I don't remember them being ornate in any way, I just saw them as something I wore when it snowed, but they were made just for me. I don't remember receiving them as a gift, but now I look at them in my mind's eye with a full heart.

My mom's mom would make us things, too. Compared to my dad's mom, grandma Helen was a slow knitter, so we would have to wait for the things she made for us, and there were times when we'd wait a year or more for a pair of her special slippers—and later in life, if you were getting married, you'd hit the mother lode and score an afghan. Every afghan she made was exactly the same, except for possibly a slight variation in the ivory color or brand of big-box store yarn (they were sturdy!), and I can say with authority that they last, as mine sits in the cabinet that holds all my linens. My sister still has hers, and I'm pretty sure my brother has his, too, and he's been married since the 1980s.

Giving and receiving isn't limited to knit items. Early on when I was sweet on a boy, I would make a tin of chocolate chip cookies and give it to my special someone. The empty tin would come back to me, and that meant I could look forward to filling it once again. For me, and I am sure for others, the act of baking is a time to ponder a friendship or feelings of love we have for someone. Or sometimes it is the gift of time we give to a loved one. It could be a few hours of sharing a skill, reading to someone who is ill, or even raising donations for the American Cancer Society when your best friend's mom is stricken with the disease.

My theory is this: We make and give gifts to others because we know how good it feels to receive a gift that was made specifically for you. It is like a giant daisy chain of giving and receiving that links us all together. Your mom/sister/grandma/friend/uncle/insert-someone-here gave something to you that they made with their hands. Their energy and care delighted you, and that energy continues on and compels us to share in turn. We make stuff. We give stuff. We make and we give and sometimes we get, and when the gifts are made by hand, everything's sweeter. And there is something meditative when it comes to making for others. It may be the repetition of the movements as with knitting, the memorized stitches repeated over and over, that lulls us into this place of thoughfulness. And in return, we receive as our own gift time to think of the person for whom we are knitting and how much we love them.

KNITTING FROM THIS BOOK

FIRST THINGS FIRST: SWATCHING? YES, PLEASE.

When you choose to knit a gift for someone else, you'll want to be extra careful to be sure it will fit and that the yarn you choose will produce an item that looks exactly the way you want it to. The two factors that will help you to achieve this are gauge and drape.

Most knitters, with some experience following a pattern, will understand what gauge is—the number of stitches and rows or rounds you get for each inch or centimeter. If your gauge matches the gauge specified in the pattern, it means the finished product will be the same size as the one in the knitting pattern. If your gauge differs by a stitch or two, and you knit a sweater, it could end up being inches larger or smaller than you intended.

Many knitters will also understand what drape is, which is how the knitted fabric behaves, bends, or lies. As far as drape is concerned, if you substitute a yarn for one that is specified in the pattern—especially if it is a different fiber—you could end up with an item that is as stiff as a board even if you started the project aiming for a nice lacy, delicate scarf. A good example is the Trellis Scarf. The pattern calls for a light, fuzzy mohair yarn. If you were to use a thin nylon yarn in its place, you would still have a beautiful scarf, but it would look entirely different—it would very likely stretch to a long and skinny piece—and the lofty lace pattern would be lost.

This is why swatching is kind of a big deal. For many knitters, swatching isn't much fun, because we may be eager to cast on and get going. If you're one of those and are willing to swatch as you knit, go for it, but promise yourself that you will dutifully unravel your project should your gauge not match the one that is called for in the pattern.

Swatching doesn't take too long. It will give you a world of information, and the info you get isn't limited to how many stitches and how many rows or rounds in one inch or centimeter. Beyond that, swatching answers questions about how the yarn and needles get along; how the resulting fabric looks, acts, and drapes; whether or not the fabric is pleasing to you; and if the yarn you chose is the right one for the project.

If you plan on making a garment, and you want the project to match the schematic given on the pattern, you will most definitely want to make a swatch to be sure that your yarn and needles produce the same row and stitch gauge. If you get more stitches per inch in your swatch, your project will be smaller than intended. If you get fewer stitches per inch, that means you'll end up with an item that is larger than intended—and you just may use more yarn than is called for in the pattern.

Items like coasters, blankets, and the like don't really require swatching, but it is still a good idea. Why? Well, first, you want to be sure that the fabric you create is pleasing, but most of all consider the fact that the yarn requirements for these patterns are dictated by the gauge listed in the pattern. That means if you don't match gauge—and especially if yours is a looser knit—you just may run out of yarn, and no one wants to find themselves in that predicament. (I always inquire about return policies when purchasing yarn, and I always buy extra—that way I can return carefully kept yarn that I haven't used but am prepared in case I need extra.)

PLANNING AHEAD

Let's face it: Knitting doesn't happen in the blink of an eye. It's not like origami, skillful as it may be, where you can whip out a piece of paper, fold it for a few minutes, and come up with a fancy crane. It's not like mixing up a batch of cookies, either, not in a million years. My grandma Helen was a slow knitter; like I said in the introduction, you'd have to wait as long as a year for a pair of her slippers (it's a good thing she sized them up; us growing children would certainly have grown out of the slippers by the time we received them). All this said, if you're someone who likes to knit gifts—and if you're reading this, chances are that you do—it makes sense to do a little common-sense planning before you settle on what to knit, who to knit for, and when to start.

Ever notice that we start seeing winter holiday ads on television and in the papers in September? In the case of television, radio, and print ads, making money is key, but there is something else at play: planning. In September, we lament the onset of winter holiday ads before autumn arrives, but when it comes to handmade items, they take time. We need time to plan, dream up ideas, and choose the perfect yarn.

Want to make your nephew a new sweater for Hanukkah? Unless he's a newborn, it could take the average knitter weeks to complete. So, it makes sense to seek out a pattern you like (there is a multisize, unisex, round-yoke pattern on page 159 that might fit the bill) and source yarn well in advance. And if you're a slowish knitter or have a limited portion of your day to knit, it makes sense to start filling out your gift-knitting calendar well in advance.

Small items like socks can take a shocking amount of time, unless you're working with a large-gauge yarn like the Slouchy Bed Socks on page 131 or the Late Summer Skimmer Socks on page 77 that are super cute and a quick knit. And if you're tight on time and decide to make up a gift for a friend whose birthday lands in April, a Trellis Scarf (page 35) will probably take a week of evenings to knit up. But if you want to knit her a full-size sweater like the Carnival Pullover on page 43, you'll want to start planning for it right before the previous year's winter holidays.

HANDMADE BASICS

CHOOSING FIBERS WISELY AND SUBSTITUTING YARN

There are times when I find a yarn, and I instinctively know what it wants to become. And there are other times when the opposite is true: I see a sweater in my head first and seek out the perfect yarn for it next. Either way, when you are knitting from a pattern, and you like the way the completed design looks in the picture and want to have that same result, you will need to use the same

yarn and achieve the same gauge. But if you substitute another yarn—especially if you are using a different fiber altogether—there is a lot more to consider than gauge, and that includes texture, fiber content, and the weight of the yarn.

To begin, take a look at the pattern and find the weight of the yarn used. If we use the Holiday Lights Sweater on page 159 as an example, note that in that pattern there is a gauge of 5 stitches per inch and that there are 220 yards to 100 grams in the Cascade 220 yarn that is used. Let's pretend that you want to swap out that yarn for one with the same gauge, but the substitute yarn has 150 yards to 50 grams. If you divide the number of grams by the number of yards, you will find that the selected yarn's weight is 0.45 grams per yard, and the one that you want to swap it for is 0.33 grams per yard. What does this mean? Well, the original yarn has a much higher weight than the substitute yarn, and even though the new yarn technically has the same gauge as the original, if you use it the sweater will be much lighter and thinner and will probably be flimsy. If this is what you're looking for, great! If your intent is to have it resemble the sweater in the picture, all bets are off. The closer your yarn is to the selected one in terms of its gauge, fiber, texture, and weight, the more successful you'll be when substituting yarn.

CAREFUL CAST-ONS AND OTHER TECHNIQUES FOR A HANDMADE LOOK

For most of us knitters, the whole arc of learning to knit most likely started out with someone showing us how to create a knit stitch, followed by a purl stitch. (Funny story—I actually know someone who remarked, during some quiet group knitting, that she'd been knitting for five years . . . and that she was finally ready to learn to purl.) Then, if we kept on knitting, we were shown how to bind off, and last we were shown how to cast on. I always wondered why things went that way, but as I sit here thinking this through, I realize that I probably wouldn't have been interested in knitting if the first thing my lovely grandma showed me was how to cast on.

Casting on isn't as much fun as, well, pretty much anything else we do that is knitting. Why? Well, for starters, it's not that easy. There's a little bit of guessing that's involved—how do I know if I've allowed enough yarn for that Long-Tail Cast-On? What happens if I run out? The list goes on. And if you aren't aware yet, guess what? There are many ways to cast on, some of them regional or individual, and many of them actually serve a particular purpose.

When it comes to making knitted gifts for friends and other loved ones, choosing the right cast-on really won't make or break the item you're gifting, but if you have a few easy tricks up your sleeve, your knits will show it. Now, I'm not going to get too fancy here by suggesting thirty-eight or so variations on the theme, but I will make a couple of suggestions to help ensure that the item you're making so carefully will look great, tidy, and finished well.

The first time you were shown how to knit, chances are you started out with the very basic Backward Loop Cast-On. It's easy to learn, but the problem with it is that it doesn't produce a very neat and tidy edge that holds up well. There are great uses for it, however. For example, it's a good choice if you are following instructions to cast on stitches at the end of a row (you will find it used in the Jelly Bean Booties on page 39). This cast-on is also used in a pinch for buttonholes when you need to cast on stitches in the middle of the row. But there are other options to explore, and I'll delve into some of them in throughout the book.

BINDING OFF

When you bind off or cast off, you are securely removing the live stitches off your needles so they don't unravel, creating a finished edge. I usually stick to one method, which is generally called a Chained Cast-Off. This is the bind-off I was taught, and I have finished my projects with this bind-off my whole knitting life (with the exception of other bind-offs that were called for in a pattern, like a Picot Bind-Off). With the Chained Cast-Off, you can bind off in pattern, which will give a ribbed edge a nice finish, since the bound-off stitches will match the row or round before. If you're comfortable with the method you're currently using and you find it gives your project a nice, even edge, there is no reason to change. One thing I do encourage, however, is to experiment while you're swatching. Some yarns behave differently, and you may find experimenting with other bind-offs or different size needles will make a difference in the finished edge.

JOINING NEW YARN AND WEAVING IN ENDS

So you've carefully cast on and have knit along happily, but you're ready to attach a new skein or change colors. There are so many ways to accomplish this, but what method will deliver the nicest and tidiest results? Short answer: Whatever way works for you and gives you the best result. Get any number of knitters together and ask them this question, and you'll get several different answers.

For me, it comes down to what fiber I'm knitting with. If I'm using 100 percent wool (but not superwash), I will simply weave in ends on the wrong side of the knitting for an inch or so one way and again the other way, then cut the yarn. As for adding a new ball of yarn, I'll spit splice, but only if the yarn and garment have a rustic nature and it'll be okay to see a puffy part of the yarn strand where it was spliced and connected together. (Or, if you tear away half the plies from each side before you spit-splice, there will be no thicker section.) Otherwise, I'll just drop the old yarn, start the new ball, and weave in the ends later. If I'm working with plied cotton, especially one with many strands, I will use knots to stop the ends from unraveling. The same goes for items made with acrylic or a natural fiber like linen. These will need to be knotted, but it isn't the end of the world. Just make sure that you're strategic about where you add a new ball of yarn, where it won't be visible: always on the wrong side and near an edge or seam.

WHAT DOES "FINISH AS DESIRED" MEAN?

You've finished the last stitch, bound off, and woven in the ends. Now what? The patterns in this book will let you know what to do once you've finished your project—to a point. You'll see that I say things like "block as desired" or "wash and block to measurements," but what exactly does this mean?

The truth is, it is up to interpretation. In other words, do what you usually do when you finish your knit. Not very helpful, right? But blocking for some knitters is a completely different activity than it is for other knitters. I have a girlfriend who owns not one set of blocking mats but three. She uses the multicolored ones for some types of knits and uses the flocked and solid-

colored ones for others. The third set? Who knows! Confession: I've been knitting and writing books professionally since 2005, and I hadn't used a blocking mat until, oh, fewer than six months ago! I never saw the point. I just spread things out nicely on a towel on a big table and if I had to, I'd pin an edge just so. And now that I think of it, drumroll and another big confession: I didn't use a blocking mat for any of the swatches that were featured in my stitch pattern books, either! (*Up, Down, All-Around Stitch Dictionary* [Abrams, 2014], T*he Knitting All Around Stitch Dictionary* [Abrams 2016], and *Japanese Stitches Unraveled* [Abrams, 2018]). In my defense, those swatches weren't gifts.

Back to finishing: Finishing means exactly what you think it means. You will launder the item (or not, if you don't feel the need) according to the ball band that came with your yarn, roll the item in a towel to get the moisture out, and lay the item out on a towel or mat on the floor, a big table, or a bed. Spread it out nicely to match the measurements in the pattern so it can dry properly. If it is a lace pattern like the Trellis Scarf on page 35 or the Cabled Table Runner on page 127, you may decide to use some pins to spread the lace pattern out or to tame any curling edges while it dries. If you have a steamer, you can always block your finished project with a bit of steam.

INCLUDING CARE INSTRUCTIONS WITH YOUR GIFTS

If your knitted gift is being given to another knitting loved one, chances are your masterpiece will be taken care of and looked after perfectly. Nonknitters, however, probably don't understand how to take care of that 100 percent wool hand-knit colorwork sweater and just may throw it in the washer and dryer along with the rest of the laundry. (You make that mistake only once in your life, right?)

Some gift givers will keep a ball band from the project and give it to the recipient so they can be sure they know how to look after their sweater, top, blanket, or cap. If you like, you can take it one step further and make a card to tuck into the package or even attach a cloth label to the inside of the garment. Quilters have been doing this for ages. As an example, you can find some cloth tape or fabric and use a washable fabric pen to write instructions on it. After finishing the edges with a zigzag sewing machine stitch, hand-tack the label to the inside of the garment. To further ensure the gift will be safe in its new owner's possession, consider giving a small bottle of wool wash or some other safe soap for laundering.

WRAPPING IT UP

Since this book and the projects in it are devoted to our four seasons, why not collect seashells to accompany a summery gift? For spring, consider fresh flowers, or use some roving to create a little nest and make blue pastel eggs to place inside. For autumn, go with pine cones, acorns, and fallen leaves, and for winter, find some fresh pine and holly or even mistletoe to embellish your gift.

Spring

is a wonderful season. This is a time when the temps are rising, the days get longer, and the snow on the ground begins to melt, revealing flower buds and growing grass. As the season begins, we throw open our windows to let the fresh air in and realize all the dreams winter promised us of venturing outside are finally coming true. Knitting is a joy this time of year because there are so many items we can make and give: colorful sweaters, fingerless mitts, little caps, lacy scarves, and cowls.

"Open your eyes to the beauty around you, open your mind to the wonders of life, open your heart to those who love you, and always be true to yourself." —MAYA ANGELOU

"It was one of those March days when the sun shines hot and the wind blows cold: when it is summer in the light, and winter in the shade." —CHARLES DICKENS

"Spring is the fountain of love for a thirsty winter." —MUNIA KHAN

"In the spring, at the end of the day, you should smell like dirt." —MARGARET ATWOOD

"Despite the forecast, live like it's spring." —LILLY PULITZER

"It is spring again. The earth / is like a child that knows poems by heart." —RAINER MARIA RILKE

ZIG ZAG WRIST WARMERS

In spring, we may get sunny skies or gray ones. The combination of yellow and gray seems to be an enduring theme. These little mitts will keep your loved ones warm in a chilly office, while taking a long walk, or while picking flowers.

FINISHED MEASUREMENTS
6 (7, 8, 9)" [15 (18, 20.5, 23) cm] hand circumference

YARN
Ewe Ewe Yarns Ewe So Sporty [100% fine superwash merino wool; 145 yards (132 meters) / 50 grams]: 1 skein each #40 Lemon Chiffon (A), #98 Charcoal (B), #97 Brushed Silver (C), and #90 Vanilla (D)

NEEDLES
One set of four or five double-pointed needles size US 3 (3.25 mm)
One set of four or five double-pointed needles size US 4 (3.5 mm)
Change needle size if necessary to obtain correct gauge.

NOTIONS
Stitch marker

GAUGE
24 sts and 32 rnds = 4" (10 cm) in Stockinette stitch (St st)

STITCH PATTERN

TWISTED RIB
(even number of sts; 1-rnd repeat)

ALL RNDS: *K1-tbl, p1; repeat from * to end.

CUFF
Using smaller needles and A, CO 36 (42, 48, 54) sts. Join for working in the rnd, being careful not to twist sts; pm for beginning of rnd.
Begin Twisted Rib; work 5 rnds even.

HAND
Change to larger needles and St st (knit all rnds); work 8 (10, 12, 12) rnds even.
Work Color Change Chart, using A as Color 1 and B as Color 2.
Cut A.
Work 6 rnds even in B.
Work Color Change Chart, using B as Color 1 and C as Color 2.
Cut B.

Work 6 rnds even in C.
Work Color Change Chart, using C as Color 1 and D as Color 2.
Cut C.
Work 6 rnds even in D.

THUMB OPENING
Change to working back and forth in rows.

ROW 1 (RS): Knit.

ROW 2: K3, purl to last 3 sts, k3.
Repeat Rows 1 and 2 seven (7, 9, 9) more times.

UPPER HAND
NEXT RND: Knit to end. Join for working in the rnd; pm for beginning of rnd.
Work 5 rnds in St st.
Change to Twisted Rib; work 5 rnds even.
BO all sts loosely in pattern.

FINISHING
Block as desired.

Color Change Chart

3

1

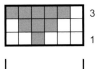

6-st repeat

☐ Knit with Color 1

■ Knit with Color 2

BUNNY EARS HAT

There's nothing cuter than a kid (or a lively teen) wearing a cap with ears. This gift takes no time at all to knit, and it's lots of fun, too, because there are so many ways to change which type of animal you're knitting. This is knit from the bottom up and in the round—a beginner knitter who knows how to work in the round will find this to be an easy knit.

Bunnies come in many colors. If you can find a heathered yarn, you can make a hat that looks like a garden rabbit. (When a yarn is heathered, it means that there is more than one color plied together. It resembles animal fur, or it looks smoky.) If you like, use white yarn for the main color and pink with a matching pink fuzzy yarn for the inner ears (even a nice ivory contrasting yarn would be fun along with the pink). You can also change the shape of the ears by following the instructions for the ears on the Foxy Poncho (page 99). That will open up a whole world of possibilities so you can create a fox, cat, dog, or raccoon!

SIZES

0–6 months (6–18 months, 18 months–4 years, 4 years–Adult Small)

FINISHED MEASUREMENTS

Approximately 16 (18¾, 20, 21¼)" [40.5 (47.5, 51, 54) cm] circumference

YARN

Morehouse Farm 3-Strand Worsted Weight Yarn [100% merino wool; 145 yards (132 meters) / 2 ounces (57 grams)]: 1 skein each Chocolate (MC) and Soft White (A); Drops Kid-Silk [75% mohair, 25% silk; 230 yards (210 meters) / 25 grams]: 1 ball #01 Off White (B)

NEEDLES

One 16" (40 cm) long circular needle size US 8 (5 mm)
Needle(s) in preferred style for small-circumference knitting in the rnd, size US 8 (5 mm)
Change needle size if necessary to obtain correct gauge.

NOTIONS

Stitch markers (including one in unique color or style for beginning of rnd)

GAUGE

18 sts and 32 rows = 4" (10 cm) in St st, using MC

STITCH PATTERN

1X1 RIB

(even number of sts; 1-rnd repeat)
ALL RNDS: *K1, p1; repeat from * to end.

PATTERN NOTE

The ears are worked using the intarsia method. You will use one strand each of A and B held together for the inside of the ears. When changing colors, bring the new yarn(s) up and to the right of the yarn(s) just used to twist the yarns and prevent leaving a hole; do not carry colors not in use across the back of the work.

HAT

Using MC and 16" (40 cm) long circular needle, CO 72 (84, 90, 96) sts. Join for working in the rnd, being careful not to twist sts; pm in a unique color or style for beginning of rnd.
Begin St st (knit every rnd); work even until piece measures 1 (1½, 2, 2½)" [2.5 (4, 5, 6.5) cm] from the beginning.

Change to 1x1 Rib; work 2 (3, 4, 4) rnds even.
Change to St st; work even until piece measures 4½ (6¾, 7½, 8½)" [11.5 (17, 19, 21.5) cm] from the beginning.
NEXT RND: Knit, decreasing 0 (4, 2, 0) sts evenly spaced—72 (80, 88, 96) sts remain.
Knit 1 rnd, pm every 9 (10, 11, 12) sts (omit last pm; beginning-of-rnd marker is here).

SHAPE CROWN

NOTE: Change to needle(s) in preferred style for small-circumference knitting in the rnd when necessary for number of sts on needle.
DECREASE RND: *Knit to 2 sts before marker, k2tog, sm; repeat from * to end—8 sts decreased.
Repeat Decrease Rnd every other rnd 7 (8, 9, 10) times—8 sts remain; 1 st remains between markers.
Knit 1 rnd, removing markers.
Cut yarn, leaving a long tail.
Thread tail through remaining sts, pull tight, and fasten off.

EARS (MAKE 2)

Using 1 strand of MC and leaving a 12" (30.5 cm) tail, CO 14 (14, 16, 16) sts; using 1 strand each of A and B held together, CO 12 (12, 14, 14) more sts—25 (26, 30, 30) sts.

ROW 1 (RS): Knit across A/B sts, knit across MC sts.

ROW 2: Purl, changing colors as established.

Repeat Rows 1 and 2 eight (8, 9, 9) more times.

SHAPE EAR

ROW 1 (RS): [K1, ssk, work to 3 sts before end of color, k2tog, k1] twice—4 sts decreased.

ROW 2: Purl.

ROW 3: Repeat Row 1—18 (18, 22, 22) sts remain.

ROW 4: Purl.

Work 2 rows even.

Repeat Rows 1 and 2 two (2, 3, 3) more times—10 sts remain.

NEXT ROW: K1, [ssk, k2tog] twice, k1—6 sts remain. Cut A/B.

With MC only, purl 1 row.

NEXT ROW: K1, ssk, k2tog, k1—4 sts remain.

Purl 1 row.

BO all sts.

FINISHING

Using MC tail, sew side ear seam. Lightly steam ears as desired. With RS facing, sew MC CO edge of ear to A/B CO edge. Pinch the bottom edge of each ear together and sew pinched edge to top of cap, beginning approximately 1" (2.5 cm) from center of crown. Block cap as desired.

TRELLIS SCARF

. . . .

Everyone has that one friend or family member who can pull off a scarf like this. It's lacy, but it has a simple and easy-to-memorize stitch pattern, so while you knit this gift, you can remember all the fun things you've done with the lucky recipient. Have a guy friend or relative who'd like a scarf similar to this? Just use their favorite color yarn and swap it with a nice, tweedy (but soft) yarn in a similar gauge—it doesn't have to be exact, though, because this scarf can be longer and wider than what you see here, and it will still be great.

FINISHED MEASUREMENTS

Approximately 7¾" (19.5 cm) wide x 45" (114.5 cm) long

YARN

Rowan Yarns Kidsilk Haze [70% mohair, 30% silk; 230 yards (210 meters) / 25 grams]: 1 ball #582 Trance

NEEDLES

One pair straight needles size US 9 (5.5 mm)
Change needle size if necessary to obtain correct gauge.

GAUGE

18 sts and 18 rows = 4" (10 cm) in Indian Pillar Stitch

SPECIAL ABBREVIATION

MAKE STAR: P3tog but do not drop sts from the needle, k2tog into the same first 2 sts, then p3tog into the same 3 sts, dropping sts off the needle.

STITCH PATTERN

INDIAN PILLAR STITCH

(multiple of 4 sts + 3; 2-row repeat)
ROW 1 (RS): K2, *make star, k1; repeat from * to last st, k1.
ROW 2: Purl.
Repeat Rows 1 and 2 for Indian Pillar Stitch.

SCARF

CO 35 sts.
Knit 2 rows.
Begin Indian Pillar Stitch; work even until piece measures approximately 45" (114.5 cm), ending with Row 1.
Knit 2 rows.
BO all sts loosely.

FINISHING

Block as desired.

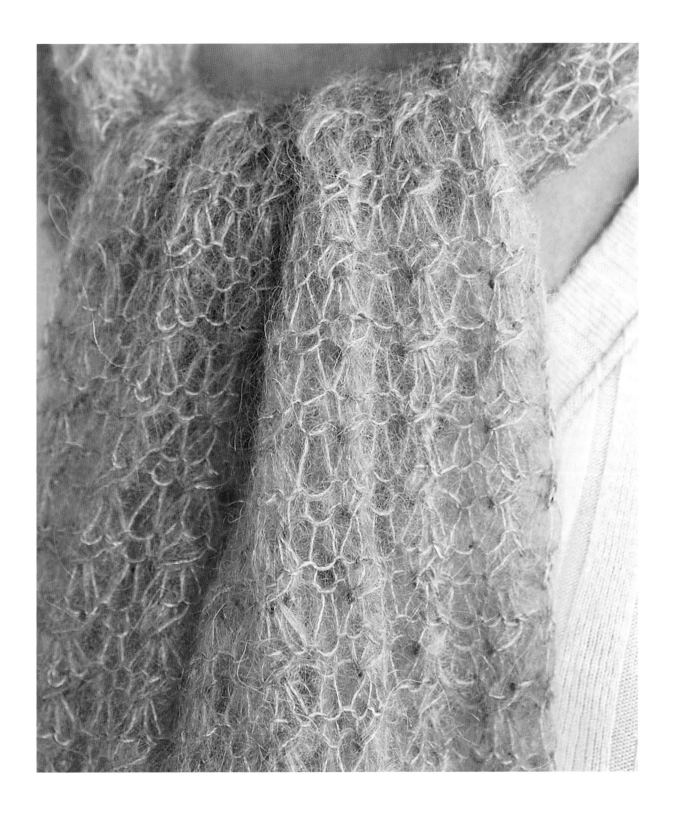

JELLY BEAN BABY BOOTIES

There's something about a beloved friend or family member who is expecting a baby—somehow the urge to knit a gift is strong! These baby booties are quick and fun to knit. They are worked flat, shaped with short rows, and seamed at the sole of the foot; they're magical, really, and what's not to love about the spring jelly bean colors?

SIZES
Newborn (3–6 months, 6 months–1 year)

FINISHED MEASUREMENTS
3½ (4¾, 5)" [9 (12, 12.5) cm] long

YARN
Scheepjes Stone Washed [78% cotton, 22% acrylic; 142 yards (130 meters) / 1.8 ounces]: 1 skein #833 Beryl, #836 Tourmaline, or #824 Turquoise

NEEDLES
One pair straight needles size US 3 (3.25 mm)
Change needle size if necessary to obtain correct gauge.

NOTIONS
Stitch markers, removable stitch marker

GAUGE
22 sts and 32 rows = 4" (10 cm) in Garter st (knit every row)

PATTERN NOTES
These booties are knit flat, then sewn together along the back of the ankle and cast-on edge. After original cast-on, use Backward Loop CO (see Special Techniques, page 168). You may make the straps longer in order to make a bow rather than a knot.

These tiny booties just beg for embellishments! Imagine little flower or animal-face buttons attached to the tops or even tiny pom-poms. And if you look at the instructions for the knitted flowers that embellish the Summer Romper on page 61, you can make those and attach them to the toes here.

FOOT

CO 19 (31, 35) sts, leaving a 10" (25.5 cm) tail.

ROW 1 (RS): K9 (15, 17), pm, k1, pm, knit to end.

ROW 2: K1-f/b, knit to marker, sm, M1L, k1, M1L, sm, knit to last st, k1-f/b—23 (35, 39) sts.

ROW 3: Knit. Place removable marker on front of piece to mark RS.

ROW 4: K1-f/b, knit to marker, sm, M1L, k3, M1L, sm, knit to last st, k1-f/b—27 (39, 43) sts.

ROW 5: Knit.

ROW 6: K1-f/b, knit to marker, sm, M1L, k1, M1L, k3, M1L, k1, M1L, sm, knit to last st, k1-f/b—33 (45, 49) sts.

ROW 7: Knit.

ROW 8: K1-f/b, knit to marker, sm, M1L, k1, M1L, k7, M1L, k1, M1L, sm, knit to last st, k1-f/b—39 (51, 55) sts.

You now have 5 Garter st ridges, including CO row.

ROWS 9–19: Knit, removing all markers on final row except for removable marker.

You now have 10 Garter st ridges.

SHAPE TOE

ROW 20 (WS): K9 (15, 17), [ssk] 5 times, k1, [k2tog] 5 times, knit to end—29 (41, 45) sts remain.

ROWS 21–23: Knit.

ROW 24: K8 (10, 11), BO 13 (21, 23) sts, knit to end—8 (10, 11) sts remain each side.

LEFT STRAP

ROW 25 (RS): K8 (10, 11), CO 25 (35, 37) sts using Backward Loop CO (see Special Techniques, page 168)—33 (45, 48) sts.

NOTE: *If you wish to tie a bow instead of a knot, CO enough sts to give you the desired strap length.*

ROWS 26 AND 27: Knit.

BO all sts. Cut yarn, leaving a 10" (25.5 cm) tail.

RIGHT STRAP

With RS facing, rejoin yarn at beginning of remaining sts.

ROW 25 (RS): P8 (10, 11), CO 25 (35, 37) sts using Backward Loop CO (see Special Techniques, page 168)—33 (45, 48) sts.

NOTE: *If you wish to tie a bow instead of a knot, CO enough sts to give you the desired strap length.*

ROWS 26 AND 27: Purl.

BO all sts.

FINISHING

With RS facing, fold piece in half widthwise. Using long tail at heel, sew heel seam, then sew halves of CO edge together. Reinforce corners between straps and foot if necessary.

CARNIVAL PULLOVER

Colorful friends and loved ones will adore this crazy sweater. It is knit from the bottom up, seamlessly, and in the round. Because the yarn is reasonably bulky, it knits up quickly and is satisfying because, after the mindless knitting of the body, there's a chunk of sweater that will steal your attention. Imagine all the color combos you can come up with. P.S. The bobbles are optional.

SIZES

To fit: 34 (36, 38, 40, 42) (44, 46, 48, 50) (52, 54, 58, 62)" [86.5 (91.5, 96.5, 101.5, 106.5) (112, 117, 122, 127) (132, 137, 147.5, 157.5) cm] chest

FINISHED MEASUREMENTS

36 (38, 40, 42, 44) (46, 48, 50, 52) (54, 56, 60, 64)" [91.5 (96.5, 101.5, 106.5, 112) (117, 122, 127, 132) (137, 142, 152.5, 162.5) cm] chest circumference

NOTE: When selecting which size to knit, choose one that is four or more inches larger than actual chest circumference.

YARN

Bartlett Yarns 2-Ply [100% wool; 210 yards (192 meters) / 4 ounces (114 grams)]: 4 (5, 5, 5, 6) (6, 6, 7, 7) (7, 8, 8, 9) skeins Natural (MC), 1 skein each Lake Blue (A), Lovat (B), Bright Orange (C), and Gold Heather (D)

NEEDLES

One 32" (80 cm) long or longer circular needle size US 8 (5 mm) Needle(s) in preferred style for small-circumference knitting in the rnd, size US 8 (5 mm) Change needle size if necessary to obtain correct gauge.

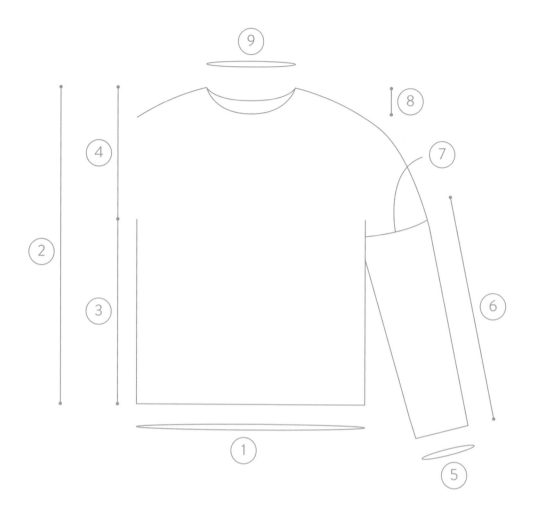

NOTIONS

Stitch markers (including one in unique color or style for beginning of rnd), waste yarn

GAUGE

16 sts and 22 rnds = 4" (10 cm) in Stockinette stitch (St st)

PATTERN NOTES

This sweater is worked in the round from the bottom up. The body is worked first, then set aside while the sleeves are worked. The pieces are then joined, and the yoke is worked in the round to the top with short-row shaping to shape the back neck.

1   36 (38, 40, 42, 44) (46, 48, 50, 52) (54, 56, 60, 64)"
    91.5 (96.5, 101.5, 106.5, 112) (117, 122, 127, 132) (137, 142, 152.5, 162.5) cm

2   14 (14, 14½, 15¼, 16) (16¼, 16½, 16¾, 17) (17¼, 17½, 17¾, 18)"
    35.5 (35.5, 37, 38.5, 40.5) (41.5, 42, 42.5, 43) (44, 44.5, 45, 45.5) cm

3   9 (9½, 10, 10¼, 10½) (10½, 10¾, 11, 11¼) (11½, 11¾, 12, 12¼)"
    23 (24, 25.5, 26, 26.5) (26.5, 27.5, 28, 28.5) (29, 30, 30.5, 31) cm

4   23 (23½, 24½, 25½, 26½) (26¾, 27¼, 27¾, 28¼) (28¾, 29¼, 29¾, 30¼)"
    58.5 (59.5, 62, 65, 67.5) (68, 69, 70.5, 72) (73, 74.5, 75.5, 77) cm

5   9½ (9½, 10, 10, 10) (11, 11, 11, 11) (11½, 11½, 11½, 11½)"
    24 (24, 25.5, 25.5, 25.5) (28, 28, 28, 28) (29, 29, 29, 29) cm

6   16¾ (17¼, 17¾, 18½, 19) (19¾, 20¼, 20½, 20½) (20¾, 20¾, 21, 21)"
    42.5 (44, 45, 47, 48.5) (50, 51.5, 52, 52) (52.5, 52.5, 53.5, 53.5) cm

7   13 (13½, 14½, 15, 15½) (16½, 17, 17½, 18½) (19, 20, 20½, 21)"
    33 (34.5, 37, 38, 39.5) (42, 43, 44.5, 47) (48.5, 51, 52, 53.5) cm

8   1"
    2.5 cm

9   15 (15, 17, 18, 19) (20, 20, 21, 22) (23, 23, 25, 27)"
    38 (38, 43, 45.5, 48.5) (51, 51, 53.5, 56) (58.5, 58.5, 63.5, 68.5) cm

BODY

Using circular needle and A, CO 144 (152, 160, 168, 176) (184, 192, 200, 208) (216, 224, 240, 256) sts. Join for working in the rnd, being careful not to twist sts; pm for beginning of rnd.

Cut A and change to MC.

Begin Garter st (knit 1 rnd, purl 1 rnd); work even for 2" (5 cm), ending with a purl rnd.

Change to St st (knit every rnd); work even until piece measures 14 (14, 14½, 15¼, 16) (16¼, 16½, 16¾, 17) (17¼, 17½, 17¾, 18)" [35.5 (35.5, 37, 38.5, 40.5) (41.5, 42, 42.5, 43) (44, 44.5, 45, 45.5) cm] from the beginning, ending 4 (4, 4, 4, 4) (6, 6, 6, 6) (6, 6, 6, 6) sts before beginning-of-rnd marker on final rnd.

DIVIDE FOR FRONT AND BACK

DIVISION RND: BO 8 (8, 8, 8, 8) (12, 12, 12, 12) (12, 12, 12, 12) sts (removing marker), k64 (68, 72, 76, 80) (80, 84, 88, 92) (96, 100, 108, 116) sts (including st on right needle after BO), BO the next 8 (8, 8, 8, 8) (12, 12, 12, 12) (12, 12, 12, 12) sts (removing marker), knit to end—64 (68, 72, 76, 80) (80, 84, 88, 92) (96, 100, 108, 116) sts remain each for front and back. Do not cut yarn; set aside, leaving sts on needle.

SLEEVES

Using needle(s) in preferred style for small-circumference knitting in the rnd and A, CO 38 (38, 40, 40, 40) (44, 44, 44, 44) (46, 46, 46, 46) sts. Join for working in the rnd, being careful not to twist sts; pm for beginning of rnd.

Cut A and change to MC.

Begin Garter st (knit 1 rnd, purl 1 rnd); work even for 2" (5 cm), ending with a purl rnd.

Change to St st.

SHAPE SLEEVE

INCREASE RND: K1, M1R, knit to last st, M1L, k1—2 sts increased.

Repeat Increase Rnd every 10 (10, 8, 8, 8) (8, 8, 6, 6) (6, 4, 4, 4) rnds 2 (6, 3, 6, 10) (7, 11, 3, 11) (11,

3, 5, 8) times, then every 12 (12, 10, 10, 0) (10, 0, 8, 8) (8, 6, 6, 6) rnds 4 (1, 5, 3, 0) (3, 0, 9, 3) (3, 13, 12, 10) time(s)—52 (54, 58, 60, 62) (66, 68, 70, 74) (76, 80, 82, 84) sts.

Work even until piece measures 16¾ (17¼, 17¾, 18½, 19) (19¾, 20¼, 20½, 20½) (20¾, 20¾, 21, 21)" [42.5 (44, 45, 47, 48.5) (50, 51.5, 52, 52) (52.5, 52.5, 53.5, 53.5) cm], ending 4 (4, 4, 4, 4) (6, 6, 6, 6) (6, 6, 6, 6) sts before beginning-of-rnd marker on final rnd.

NEXT RND: BO 8 (8, 8, 8, 8) (12, 12, 12, 12) (12, 12, 12, 12) sts (removing marker), knit to end—44 (46, 50, 52, 54) (54, 56, 58, 62) (64, 68, 70, 72) sts remain. Cut yarn, transfer sts to waste yarn, and set aside.

Repeat for second sleeve, leaving sts on needle(s).

YOKE

JOINING RND: With RS facing, using circular needle and yarn attached to body, knit across 44 (46, 50, 52, 54) (54, 56, 58, 62) (64, 68, 70, 72) left sleeve sts, pm, knit across 64 (68, 72, 76, 80) (80, 84, 88, 92) (96, 100, 108, 116) front sts pm, knit across 44 (46,

50, 52, 54) (54, 56, 58, 62) (64, 68, 70, 72) right sleeve sts, pm, then knit across 64 (68, 72, 76, 80) (80, 84, 88, 92) (96, 100, 108, 116) back sts, place unique marker for beginning of rnd—216 (228, 244, 256, 268) (268, 280, 292, 308) (320, 336, 356, 376) sts.

NEXT RND: Knit, decreasing a total of 0 (0, 4, 4, 4) (4, 4, 4, 2) (2, 0, 2, 4) sts evenly spaced, working the decreases right before or after sleeve markers—216 (228, 240, 252, 264) (264, 276, 288, 306) (318, 336, 354, 372) sts. Knit 1 rnd.

Begin Chart A; work Rnds 1–5 once. Cut MC and B.

Continuing with C, work even until piece measures 2 (2¼, 2¼, 2½, 2½) (2½, 2½, 2½, 2¾) (2¾, 3, 3, 3)" [5 (5.5, 5.5, 6.5, 6.5) (6.5, 6.5, 6.5, 7) (7, 7.5, 7.5, 7.5) cm] from Joining Rnd.

SHAPE YOKE AND WORK CHARTS
NOTE: When working decreases across a marker, replace the marker after working the decrease.
Sizes 34, 36, 38, 42, 44, 48, 52, 54, 58, and 62" Only:
DECREASE RND 1: *K2tog, k4 (2, 3,

-, 2) (2, -, 2, -) (-, 2, 2, 4), [k2tog, k3 (3, 0, -, 3) (3, -, 3, -) (-, 3, 3, 3)] 6 (3, 0, -, 8) (8, -, 4, -) (-, 2, 11, 5) times; repeat from * to end—174 (180, 192, -, 210) (210, -, 228, -) (-, 264, 282, 300) sts remain.
Sizes 40, 46, 50, and 52" Only:
DECREASE RND 1: *[K2tog, k2] - (-, -, 3, -) (-, 4, -, 4) (2, -, -, -) times, [k2tog, k3] - (-, -, 6, -) (-, 6, -, 7) (9, -, -, -) times; repeat from * to end— - (-, -, 198, -) (-, 216, -, 240) (252, -, -, -) sts remain.
All Sizes: Begin Chart B; work Rnds 1–3 once. Cut C.

Continuing with D, work even until piece measures 4 (4½, 4½, 4¾, 5) (5, 5, 5, 5¼) (5½, 5½, 5¾, 5¾)" [10 (11.5, 11.5, 12, 12.5) (12.5, 12.5, 12.5, 13.5) (14, 14, 14.5, 14.5) cm] from Joining Rnd.

DECREASE RND 2: *[K2tog, k3 (3, 2, 3, 3) (3, 2, 3, 3) (3, 2, 3, 2)] 1 (2, 1, 1, 3) (3, 2, 2, 4) (1, 1, 3, 5) time(s), [k2tog, k2 (2, 0, 2, 2) (2, 0, 2, 2) (2, 0, 2, 3)] 6 (5, 0, 7, 5) (5, 0, 7, 5) (4, 0, 8, 6) times; repeat from * to end—132 (138, 144, 150, 162) (162, 162, 174, 186) (192, 198, 216, 234) sts remain.

Begin Chart C; work Rnds 1–3 once. Cut A and D.

Change to MC; work even until piece measures 6 (6½, 6¾, 7, 7¼)

(7¼, 7½, 7½, 7¾) (7¾, 8, 8, 8¼)"
[15 (16.5, 17, 18, 18.5) (18.5, 19, 19,
19.5) (19.5, 20.5, 20.5, 21) cm]
from Joining Rnd.

DECREASE RND 3: *[K2tog, k2 (0, 2,
1, 2) (1, 1, 1, 2) (1, 2, 2, 2)] 1 (1, 3, 3,
3) (1, 1, 3, 4) (4, 3, 3, 3) time(s),
[k2tog, k1 (1, 1, 2, 1) (2, 2, 2, 1) (2,
1, 1, 1)] 6 (7, 4, 4, 5) (6, 6, 5, 5) (5,
7, 8, 9) time(s); repeat from * to
end—90 (90, 102, 108, 114) (120,
120, 126, 132) (138, 138, 150, 162)
sts remain.
Begin Chart A; work Rnds 1–5
once. Cut B.
Continuing in C, knit 1 rnd.
NEXT RND: *With C k2, with D k1;
repeat from * to end. Cut C.
NEXT RND: *With MC k2, with D k1;
repeat from * to end.
Work even with MC until piece
measures 8 (8½, 9, 9¼, 9½) (9½,
9¾, 10, 10¼) (10½, 10¾, 11, 11¼)"
[20.5 (21.5, 23, 23.5, 24) (24, 25,
25.5, 26) (26.5, 27.5, 28, 28.5)
cm] from Joining Rnd. Cut D.
Continue in MC for remainder of
piece.

Chart A

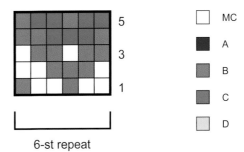

6-st repeat

Chart B

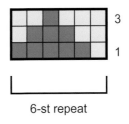

6-st repeat

Chart C

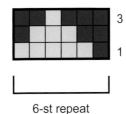

6-st repeat

SHAPE NECK

NOTE: Neck is shaped using short rows (see Special Techniques, page 171).

SHORT ROW 1 (RS): Work to third marker (end of right sleeve), sm, w&t.

SHORT ROW 2 (WS): Sm, purl to third marker (end of left sleeve), sm, w&t.

SHORT ROW 3: Knit to 6 sts before wrapped st from previous RS row, w&t.

SHORT ROW 4: Purl to 6 sts before wrapped st from previous WS row, w&t.

SHORT ROW 5: Knit to end.

Knit 1 rnd, working wraps together with wrapped sts as you come to them.

DECREASE RND 4: *K2tog, k1; repeat from * to end—60 (60, 68, 72, 76) (80, 80, 84, 88) (92, 92, 100, 108) sts remain.

Begin 1x1 Rib; work even for 1" (2.5 cm).

BO all sts loosely.

FINISHING

Using yarn tails, sew underarm sts.

BOBBLES

Make bobbles as follows: Using A, CO 1 st, leaving an 8" (20.5 cm) tail.

[(K1-f/b) 3 times, k1-f] into 1 st to increase to 7 sts, turn; p7, pulling yarn tight on first st, turn; k2tog, slip st back to left needle and pass 2nd, 3rd, 4th, 5th, then 6th sts over first st—1 st remains. Cut yarn, leaving an 8" (20.5 cm) tail, and fasten. Sew bobbles to RS, evenly spaced around, between Charts C and A (see photos), securing bobbles in place on WS. Block as desired.

NAUTICAL STRIPE COWL

Spring marks the beginning of outdoor fun in the sun and by the oceans and seas, and that is likely why we revisit nautical themes at this time every year. This striped cowl is a fun knit—it's worked in a tube and in the round—and you can whip this up in no time. To kick it up a notch, imagine if you just used scraps that you have in your stash. You could make a crazy color version of this any time of year, and it would be such a fun gift.

FINISHED MEASUREMENTS
5¾" (14.5 cm) width x 31" (78.5 cm) circumference

YARN
Berroco Modern Cotton DK [60% pima cotton, 40% modal rayon; 335 yards (306 meters) / 100 grams]: 1 hank each #6663 Hope (navy) (A) and #6600 Bluffs (white) (B)

NEEDLES
One set of four or five double-pointed needles size US 5 (3.75 mm)

Two spare circular needles in any length, size US 5 (3.75 mm) or one size smaller, for finishing Change needle size if necessary to obtain correct gauge.

NOTIONS
Stitch marker, crochet hook size US F-5 (3.75 mm)

GAUGE
23 sts and 32 rnds = 4" (10 cm) in Stockinette stitch (St st)

PATTERN NOTES

This cowl begins with a provisional cast-on; when the cowl is complete, the cast-on edge is joined to the live stitches using Kitchener stitch. If you prefer, you may cast on using your favorite cast-on, bind off the end of the cowl, then sew the edges together.

When changing colors in the stripe pattern, carry the color not in use up the inside of the cowl if it will be used again in 5 rounds or fewer. Otherwise, cut the yarn. Weave in ends as you go.

COWL

Using Provisional CO (see Special Techniques, page 170) and A, CO 65 sts. Join for working in the rnd, being careful not to twist sts; pm for beginning of rnd.

Begin St st (knit every rnd); work 2 rnds.

Change to B; work 2 rnds.

Change to A; work 2 rnds.

Repeat last 4 rnds until piece measures 13" (33 cm) from the beginning, ending with 2 rnds of A.

Continuing in B, work 6" (15 cm).

Change to A; work 10 rnds.

Change to B; work 7 rnds.

Repeat last 17 rnds until striped section measures approximately 12" (30.5 cm) and piece measures approximately 31" (78.5 cm), ending with 7 rnds of B. Cut yarn, leaving a tail approximately 4 times the circumference of the piece.

FINISHING

Weave in remaining ends. Transfer live sts to one spare circular needle. Carefully unzip provisional CO and place sts on second spare circular needle. Bring tube ends together, matching up first and last sts so that tube isn't twisted. Using Kitchener st, graft ends together. Block as desired.

Summer is the time for

road trips, hikes, picnics, and hanging out at the lake, the beach, or the backyard pool. School has ended, and we hear children playing outside late into the afternoon and evening. Our knit garments are put away for now, but not entirely. We are drawn to knitting smaller projects and take-along projects like socks and whimsical goodies, and sleeveless tops and tanks that will keep us cool.

"Bees do have a smell, you know, and if they don't they should, for their feet are dusted with spices from a million flowers." —RAY BRADBURY

"I have only to break into the tightness of a strawberry, and I see summer—its dust and lowering skies." —TONI MORRISON

"It was June, and the world smelled of roses. The sunshine was like powdered gold over the grassy hillside." —MAUD HART LOVELACE

"Sweet, sweet burn of sun and summer wind, and you my friend, my new fun thing, my summer fling." —K.D. LANG

"The dandelions and buttercups / Gild all the lawn; the drowsy bee / Stumbles among the clover-tops, / And summer sweetens all but me." —JAMES RUSSELL LOWELL

MERMAID TAIL LAP BLANKET

....

When I was little and if I couldn't sleep, I would read the works of Hans Christian Andersen over and over and loved "The Little Mermaid" most of all. Now, there's a Disney version, but the idea of having a cozy shaped like a mermaid's tail would've been heaven on earth for me. This is knit in the round, and the fins are knit separately and added on later. This is sized so you can make one for a big kid, too.

SIZES
Small (Large)
To fit ages 3–10 (12 and up)

FINISHED MEASUREMENTS
Circumference: Approximately 29¾ (48½)" [75.5 (123) cm]
Length: 32¼ (45½)" [82 (115.5) cm], not including fins

YARN
Berroco Comfort Chunky [50% super fine acrylic, 50% super fine nylon; 150 yards (138 meters) / 3½ ounces (100 grams)]: 4 (8) skeins #5717 Raspberry Coulis

NEEDLES
One 24" (60 cm) long or longer circular needle size US 10 (6 mm)
One set of four or five double-pointed needles and one 24" (60 cm) long or longer circular needle size US 10½ (6.5 mm)
One pair straight needles size US 11 (8 mm)
Change needle size if necessary to obtain correct gauge.

NOTIONS
Stitch markers

GAUGE
14 sts and 18 rnds = 4" (10 cm) in Stockinette stitch (St st), using larger needle

SPECIAL ABBREVIATION

Sp2p (double decrease): Slip the next stitch purlwise to the right-hand needle, p2tog, pass the slipped stitch over the stitch from the p2tog.

STITCH PATTERN

SHADOW RIB

(multiple of 3 sts; 2-rnd repeat)

RND 1: P1, *k1-tbl, p2; repeat from * to last 2 sts, k1-tbl, p1.

RND 2: Purl.

Repeat Rnds 1 and 2 for Shadow Rib.

PATTERN NOTES

The tail is worked in the round from the waist to the end, leaving a hole at the bottom end. The fins are worked separately, then sewn together. One end is inserted into the bottom opening of the tail, and the pieces are sewn together.

TAIL

Using smaller circular needle, CO 105 (171) sts. Join for working in the rnd, being careful not to twist sts; pm for beginning of rnd. Knit 1 rnd.

Begin Shadow Rib; work even until piece measures 3 (3½)" [7.5 (9) cm], ending with Rnd 1 of pattern.

Change to larger circular needle and St st (knit every rnd), decreasing 1 st on first rnd—104 (170) sts remain.

Work even until piece measures 20 (25)" [51 (63.5) cm] from the beginning. Place marker after 52 (85) sts.

SHAPE LOWER TAIL

NOTE: Change to dpns when necessary for number of sts on needle.

DECREASE RND: [K1, k2tog, knit to 3 sts before marker, ssk, k1, sm] twice—4 sts decreased.

SIZE SMALL ONLY: Repeat Decrease Rnd every 3 rnds 18 more times—28 sts remain.

SIZE LARGE ONLY: *Repeat Decrease Rnd every other rnd once, then every 3 rnds twice.

Repeat from * 10 more times, then repeat Decrease Rnd every 3 rnds once more—30 sts remain.

BOTH SIZES: Set aside, leaving sts on needle.

FINS (MAKE 2)

Using larger straight needles, CO 7 sts, leaving a 10" (25.5 cm) tail.

TOP SECTION

ROW 1 (RS): K1, p1, [k1-f/b] twice, k1, p2—9 sts.

ROW 2: *P1, k1; repeat from * to last st, k1.

ROW 3: K1, p1, k1, p1-f/b, k1-f/b, p1, k1, p2—11 sts.

ROW 4: [P1, k1] twice, p3, k1, p1, k2.

ROW 5: [K1, p1] twice, [k1-f/b] twice, k1, p1, k1, p2—13 sts.

ROW 6: Repeat Row 2.

ROW 7: [K1, p1] twice, k1, p1-f/b, k1-f/b, [p1, k1] twice, p2—15 sts.

ROW 8: [P1, k1] 3 times, p3, [k1, p1] twice, k2.

ROW 9: [K1, p1] 3 times, [k1-f/b] twice, [k1, p1] twice, k1, p2—17 sts.

ROW 10: Repeat Row 2.

ROW 11: [K1, p1] 3 times, k1, p1-f/b, k1-f/b, [p1, k1] 3 times, p2—19 sts.

ROW 12: [P1, k1] 4 times, p3, [k1, p1] 3 times, k2.

ROW 13: [K1, p1] 4 times, [k1-f/b] twice, [k1, p1] 3 times, k1, p2—21 sts.

ROW 14: Repeat Row 2.

CENTER SECTION

ROW 15: K1, p2tog, [p1, k1] 3 times, p1-f/b, k1-f/b, [p1, k1] 3 times, p1, p2tog, p1.

ROW 16: P1, k2, [p1, k1] 3 times, p3, [k1, p1] 4 times, k3.

ROW 17: K1, p2tog, [k1, p1] 3 times, [k1-f/b] twice, [k1, p1] 3 times, k1, p2tog, p1.

ROW 18: Repeat Row 2.

Repeat Rows 15–18 two (4) more times.

BOTTOM SECTION

ROW 1: K1, ssp, [p1, k1] 3 times, p1-f/b, k1-f/b, [p1, k1] 3 times, p1, p2tog, p1.

ROW 2: P1, k2tog, [p1, k1] 3 times, p3, [k1, p1] 3 times, ssk, k1—19 sts.

ROW 3: K1, ssp, [p1, k1] twice, p1, [k1-f/b] twice, [k1, p1] 3 times, p2tog, p1.

ROW 4: P1, k2tog, [p1, k1] 6 times, p1, k2tog, k1—17 sts.

ROW 5: K1, ssp, [p1, k1] twice, p1-f/b, k1-f/b, [p1, k1] twice, p1, p2tog, p1.

ROW 6: P1, k2tog, [p1, k1] twice, p2, [p1, k1] twice, p1, ssk, k1—15 sts.

ROW 7: K1, ssp, p1, k1, p1, [k1-f/b] twice, [k1, p1] twice, p2tog, p1.

ROW 8: P1, k2tog, [p1, k1] 4 times, p1, ssk, k1—13 sts.

ROW 9: K1, ssp, p1, k1, p1-f/b, k1-f/b, p1, k1, p1, p2tog, p1.

ROW 10: P1, k2tog, p1, k1, p3, k1, p1, ssk, k1—11 sts.

ROW 11: K1, ssp, p1, [k1-f/b] twice, k1, p1, p2tog, p1.

ROW 12: P1, k2tog, [p1, k1] twice, p1, ssk, k1—9 sts.

ROW 13: K1, ssp, sk2p, p2tog, p1—5 sts.

ROW 14: P1, sp2p, k1—3 sts.

ROW 15: K2, p1.

ROW 16: P2, k1.

Cut yarn, leaving an 8" (20.5 cm) tail; thread tail through remaining sts, and pull tight into a point.

FINISHING

Lay fins RS up and side by side, with pointed ends at the bottom. Using one of the yarn tails and beginning at CO edge, whipstitch adjacent side edges of fins together for approximately 2–3" (5–7.5 cm).

Return to tail sts on circular needle. Cut yarn, leaving a 30" (76 cm) tail. Thread tail through sts, removing needle as you go. Do not cinch up sts.

Turn tail inside out and lay flat with shaped edges along outside edges. Place sewn fins inside tail, with CO edge of fins aligned with and sandwiched between both layers of live tail sts. Cinch tail sts if necessary until they are the same width as the top of the fins. Starting on either end of live tail sts, sew through all 3 thicknesses (2 layers of live tail sts and one layer of fins) with whipstitch or running st.

Turn RS out.

If desired, when blocking, pin the fins so that they spread open.

SUMMER ROMPER

It's always so much fun to knit for toddlers! This little romper can be made as-is, with added extra flowers, or even in plain Stockinette stitch with stripes. If you want to gift a complete outfit, buy an extra ball of yarn and make the Jelly Bean Booties on page 39 to match.

SIZES
3 months (6 months, 12 months)

FINISHED MEASUREMENTS
Hip circumference: 21¼ (22¾, 24½)" [54 (58, 62) cm]
Chest circumference: 19 (20½, 22)" [48.5 (52, 56) cm]

YARN
Bernat Softee Baby Cotton [60% cotton, 40% acrylic; 254 yards (232 meters) / 4.2 ounces (120 grams)]: 3 (3, 4) balls Feather Gray (MC)

NEEDLES
One 16" (40 cm) long circular needle size US 5 (3.75 mm)
One pair straight needles size US 4 (3.5 mm)
Change needle size if necessary to obtain correct gauge.

NOTIONS
Stitch markers, stitch holder or waste yarn, three ½" (1.5 mm) shank buttons, two ½" (1.5 mm) flat buttons

GAUGE
22 sts and 29 rnds = 4" (10 cm) in St st, using larger needle and MC
21 sts and 32 rnds = 4" (10 cm) in Box Stitch, using larger needle and MC

SPECIAL ABBREVIATION
DEC1: Decrease 1 st in pattern, working k2tog if next st in

pattern is a knit st, or p2tog if next st in pattern is a purl st.

STITCH PATTERN

BOX STITCH
(multiple of 4 sts; 4-rnd repeat)
RNDS 1 AND 2: *K2, p2; repeat from * to end.
RNDS 3 AND 4: *P2, k2; repeat from * to end.
Repeat Rnds 1–4 for Box Stitch.

PATTERN NOTES
This pattern begins with the front and back tabs at the crotch, which are then joined for the body. The body is worked in the round to the beginning of the bib, then divided for front and back, which are worked separately to the end.
After the original cast-on, use Backward Loop Cast-On (see Special Techniques, page 168) for all remaining cast-ons.

BACK TAB
Using larger needle and MC, CO 18 (20, 22) sts.
Purl 6 (6, 8) rows.

SHAPE BOTTOM
Continuing in Garter st (purl every row), and using Backward Loop CO (see Special Techniques, page 168), CO 2 sts at end of next 2 rows, 4 sts at end of next 6 (4, 4) rows, 3 sts at end of next 2 (4, 6) rows, then 2 sts at end of next 2 (4, 2) rows—56 (60, 64) sts.
Transfer sts to st holder or waste yarn.

FRONT TAB
Using larger needle and MC, CO 18 (20, 22) sts.
Purl 3 rows.
BUTTONHOLE ROW: *P3, yo, p2tog; repeat from * to last 3 sts, p3.
Purl 8 (8, 10) rows.

SHAPE BOTTOM
Continuing in Garter st, CO 2 sts at end of next 2 (4, 4) rows, 6 (5, 6) sts at end of next 2 rows, then 11 sts at end of next 2 rows—56 (60, 64) sts.

BODY

JOIN BACK AND FRONT TABS
Purl to end of front sts, pm, purl across back sts from holder—108 sts. Join for working in the rnd; pm for beginning of rnd.
Purl 1 rnd.
Begin Box st; work even until body measures 5¾ (7¼, 9)" [14.5 (18.5, 23) cm] from beginning of Box st.

SHAPE BODY
DECREASE RND: [Work 1 st in pattern, dec1, work to 3 sts before marker, dec1, work 1 st in pattern, sm] twice—4 sts decreased.
Continuing in pattern as established, repeat Decrease Rnd every 5th rnd 2 more times—100 (108, 116) sts remain.
Work even through Rnd 2 or 4 of pattern.

BIB
RND 1: [P4, knit to 4 sts before marker, p4, sm] twice.
RND 2: Knit.
Repeat Rnds 1 and 2 four more times.

DIVIDE FOR FRONT AND BACK
Transfer last 50 (54, 58) sts of rnd to st holder or waste yarn for back, removing markers—50 (54, 58) sts remain for front.

FRONT

SHAPE FRONT
ROW 1 (RS): P4, ssk, knit to last 6 sts, k2tog, p4—2 sts decreased.
ROW 2: K4, purl to last 4 sts, k4.
Repeat Rows 1 and 2 eight more times—32 (34, 36) sts remain.
Change to Garter st across all

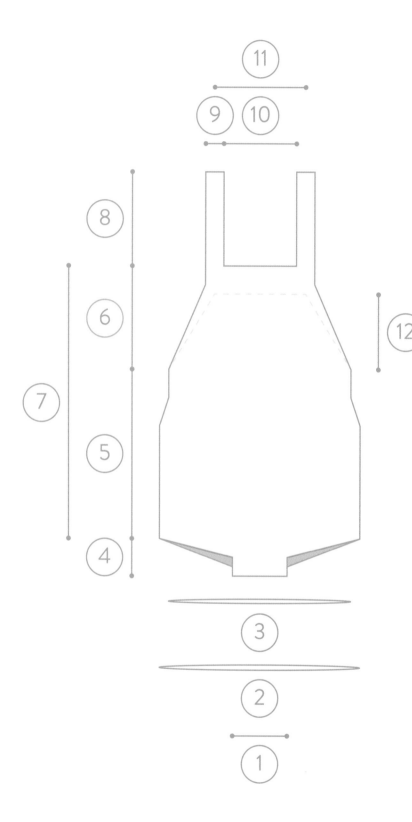

1   3¼ (3¾, 4)"
    8.5 (9.5, 10) cm

2   21¼ (22¾, 24½)"
    54 (58, 62) cm

3   19 (20½, 22)"
    48.5 (52, 56) cm

4   1¾ (2, 2¼)"
    4.5 (5, 5.5) cm

5   9½ (11½, 13½)"
    24 (29, 34.5) cm

6   4¾ (5¼, 5¾)"
    12 (13.5, 14.5) cm

7   14¼ (16¾, 19¼)"
    36 (42.5, 49) cm

8   5¼ (6¼, 7¼)"
    13.5 (16, 18.5)

9   ¾"
    2 cm

10 4¼ (4¾, 5)"
    11 (12, 12.5) cm

11 5½ (5¾, 6¼)" top of back
    14 (14.5, 16) cm

12 3¾ (4¼, 4½)" back bib length
    9.5 (11, 11.5) cm

sts (purl every row); work 8 rows even.

STRAPS

NEXT ROW (RS): P4 and place on st holder or waste yarn, BO the next 24 (26, 28) sts, purl to end—4 sts remain.

Working on one strap, continue in Garter st (knit every row) until piece measures 3½ (4½, 5½)" [9 (11.5, 14) cm] from division, ending with a RS row.

BUTTONHOLE ROW 1 (WS): K1, k2tog, yo, k1.

Work 1" (2.5 cm) even, ending with a RS row.

BUTTONHOLE ROW 1 (WS): K1, yo, k2tog, k1.

Work even until piece measures 5¼ (6¼, 7¼)" [13.5 (16, 18.5) cm] from division.

Rejoin yarn to sts on hold for second strap. Complete as for first strap.

BACK

With RS facing, rejoin yarn to sts on hold for back.

SHAPE BACK

ROW 1 (RS): P4, ssk, knit to last 6 sts, k2tog, p4—2 sts decreased.

ROW 2: K4, purl to last 4 sts, k4.

Repeat Rows 1 and 2 nine (10,

11) more times—30 (32, 34) sts remain.
Change to Garter st across all sts; work 8 rows even.
BO all sts.

FLOWERS

(optional; make as many as desired)

SMALL FLOWER

Using larger needle and MC, CO 36 sts.
NEXT ROW: *K1, BO the next 4 sts (there is now 1 st left on the RH needle); repeat from * to end—12 sts remain.

Cut yarn, leaving a 10" (25.5 cm) tail; thread tail through remaining sts, pull tight, and fasten off.

LARGE FLOWER

Using larger needle and MC, CO 70 sts.
NEXT ROW: *K1, BO the next 5 sts (1 st left on right needle after BO); repeat from * to end—20 sts remain.
Cut yarn, leaving a 10" (25.5 cm) tail; thread tail through remaining sts, pull tight, and fasten off.
Sew flowers in place (see photos) using tails; bring tails to WS and secure.

FINISHING

LEG EDGING

With RS facing, using smaller needles and MC, pick up and knit approximately 52 (54, 58) sts along one leg opening from tab to tab. Knit 3 rows. BO all sts knitwise. Repeat for opposite leg opening.
Sew 3 shank buttons to RS of back tab, opposite buttonholes on front tab.
Sew flat buttons on WS of back, one at each top corner. Straps will fasten to these buttons on the inside of the romper.

SAND DOLLAR LACE TOP

This summery round-yoke tee is knit top down and in one piece with an easy-to-memorize lace pattern. Knitting top down makes it an easy gift because its construction allows for on-the-fly adaptations. Want to make a longer sleeve? Just continue knitting each sleeve until it is the length you want. Same goes for the depth of the neckline: If you want to make it shorter, just join the yoke and work in rounds when it is the depth you like. Alternatively, you can make it deeper by working the yoke flat a little longer. (When making adaptations, always make sure you have extra yarn on hand.)

SIZES

To fit: 28 (32, 36, 40) (44, 48, 52)" [71 (81.5, 91.5, 101.5) (112, 122, 132) cm] chest

NOTE: Intended to be worn with 2" (5 cm) ease; for greater ease, consider working one size larger.

FINISHED MEASUREMENTS

30½ (34¼, 38½, 42¼) (46½, 50¼, 54½)" [77.5 (87, 98, 107.5) (118, 127.5, 138.5) cm] chest circumference

YARN

Cascade Yarns Ultra Pima [100% pima cotton; 220 yards (200 meters) / 3½ ounces (100 grams)]: 3 (4, 4, 4) (5, 5, 6) hanks #3759 Taupe

NEEDLES

One 24" (60 cm) long circular needle size US 6 (4.25 mm) Needle(s) in preferred style for small-circumference knitting in the rnd, size US 6 (4.25 mm) Change needle size if necessary to obtain correct gauge.

NOTIONS

Stitch markers, waste yarn

GAUGE

22 sts and 28 rnds = 4" (10 cm) in St st

STITCH PATTERN

FAGGOTING

(even number of sts; 1-rnd repeat)

ALL ROWS: K1, *yo, ssk; repeat from * to last st, k1.

PATTERN NOTES

This sweater is worked in one piece from the top down to the underarms, then body and sleeves are worked separately in the round to the bottom edge.

YOKE

Using circular needle, CO 68 (76, 76, 80) (84, 88, 88) sts. Do not join.

SET-UP ROW (RS): K4, pm, knit to last 4 sts, pm, k4.

Knit 7 rows.

Sizes 28, 44, 48, and 52" Only:

INCREASE ROW 1 (RS): K4, sm, *[k1-f/b, k2] 1 (-, -, -) (1, 2, 2) time(s), [k1-f/b, k1] 6 (-, -, -) (8, 7, 7) times; repeat from * to marker, sm, k4—96 (-, -, -) (120, 124, 124) sts.

Sizes 32, 36, and 40" Only:

INCREASE ROW 1 (RS): K4, sm, [k1-f/b, k- (1, 1, 2) (-, -, -)] 2 times, *k1-f/b, k1, k1-f/b, k2; repeat from * to - (4, 4, 6) (-, -, -) sts before marker, [k1-f/b, k- (1, 1, 2) (-, -, -)] twice, sm, k4— - (104, 104, 104) (-, -, -) sts.

All Sizes:

Work 5 rows in Faggoting, keeping first and last 4 sts in Garter st (knit every row).

Knit 4 rows.

Sizes 28 and 44" Only:

INCREASE ROW 2 (RS): K4, sm, *k1-f/b, k2, [k1-f/b, k1] 4 (-, -, -) (2, -, -) times; repeat from * to marker, sm, k4—136 (-, -, -) (168, -, -) sts.

Sizes 32, 36, 40, 48 and 52" Only:

INCREASE ROW 2 (RS): K4, sm, [k1-f/b, k1] - (2, 2, 3) (-, 1, 1) time(s), *k1-f/b, k2, [k1-f/b, k1] - (4, 4, 4) (-, 2, 2) times; repeat from * to marker, sm, k4— - (148, 148, 154) (-, 174, 174) sts.

All Sizes:

Work 5 rows in Faggoting, keeping first and last 4 sts in Garter st.

Knit 4 rows.

Sizes 28, 36, and 44" Only:

INCREASE ROW 3 (RS): K4, sm, *k1-f/b, k1; repeat from * to marker, sm, k4—200 (-, 218, -) (248, -, -) sts.

Sizes 32, 48, and 52" Only:

INCREASE ROW 3 (RS): K4, sm, [k1-f/b, k1] - (1, -, -) (-, 3, 1) time(s), *k1-f/b, k- (2, -, -) (-, 0, 0), [k1-f/b, k1] - (8, -, -) (-, 6, 4) times; repeat from * to marker, sm, k4— - (214, -, -) (-, 264, 266) sts.

Size 40" Only:

INCREASE ROW 3 (RS): K4, sm, k1-f/b, k2, *k1-f/b, k1; repeat from * to 3 sts before marker, k1-f/b, k2, sm, k4—226 sts.

All Sizes:

Work 5 rows in Faggoting, keeping first and last 4 sts in Garter st.

Knit 4 rows.

Sizes 28, 44, and 48" Only:

INCREASE ROW 4 (RS): K4, sm, *[k1-f/b, k4 (-, -, -) (3, 1, -)] 4 (-, -, -) (3, 1, -) time(s), [k1-f/b, k3 (-, -, -) (2, 2, -)] 7 (-, -, -) (4, 10, 0) times; repeat from * to marker, sm, k4— 244 (-, -, -) (318, 352, -) sts.

Sizes 32, 40, and 52" Only:

INCREASE ROW 4 (RS): K4, sm, k1-f/b, k- (3, -, 3) (-, -, 2), *k1-f/b, k- (4, -, 3) (-, -, 1), [k1-f/b, k- (3, -, 2) (-, -, 2)] - (1, -, 1) (-, -, 4) time(s); repeat from * to - (8, 0, 8) (-, -, 7) sts before marker, k1-f/b, k- (3, -, 3) (-, -, 2), sm, k4— - (260, -, 288) (-, -, 358) sts.

Size 36" Only:

INCREASE ROW 4 (RS): K4, sm,

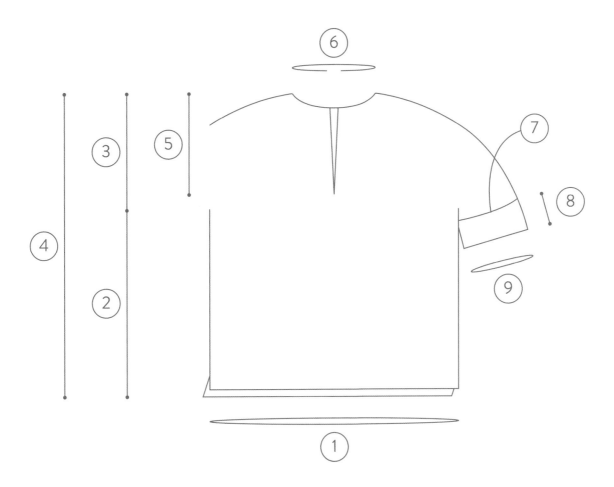

1   30½ (34¼, 38½, 42¼) (46½, 50¼, 54½)"
20.5   77.5 (87, 98, 107.5) (118, 127.5, 138.5) cm

2   13 (13, 13½, 13) (13½, 13½, 13½)"
33 (33, 34.5, 33) (34.5, 59.5, 34.5) cm

3   8 (8½, 8½, 9) (9½, 10, 10½)"
20.5 (21.5, 21.5, 23) (24, 25.5, 26.5) cm

4   21 (21½, 22, 22) (23, 23½, 24)"
53.5 (54.5, 56, 56) (58.5, 59.5, 61) cm

5   7 (7, 7½, 8) (8, 8, 8)"
18 (18, 19, 20.5) (20.5, 20.5, 20.5) cm

6   12¼ (13¾, 13¾, 14½) (15¼, 16, 16)"
31 (35, 35, 37) (38.5, 40.5, 40.5) cm

7   10 (10½, 11¾, 13) (14¼, 16, 17)"
25.5 (26.5, 30, 33) (36, 40.5, 43) cm

8   2¼ (2¼, 2¼, 2¼) (2¼, 2¼, 2¼)"
5.5 (5.5, 5.5, 5.5) (5.5, 5.5, 5.5) cm

9   9¼ (9¾, 11, 12¼) (13¾, 15¼, 16¼)"
23.5 (25, 28, 31) (35, 38.5, 41.5) cm

k1-f/b, k4, *k1-f/b, k3; repeat from * to marker, sm, k4—270 sts.

All Sizes:

Knit 2 rows.

Purl 1 row, keeping first and last 4 sts in Garter st.

Sizes 28, 40, and 48" Only:

INCREASE ROW 5 (RS): K4, sm, [k1-f/b, k23 (-, -, 11) (-, 12, -)] 1 (-, -, 2) (-, 1, -) time(s), *k1-f/b, k23 (-, -, 12) (-, 13, -), [k1-f/b, k22 (-, -, 11) (-, 12, -)] 1 (-, -, 4) (-, 3, -) time(s); repeat from * to 24 (-, -, 12) (-, 13, -) sts before marker, k1-f/b, k23 (-, -, 11) (-, 12, -), sm, k4—254 (-, -, 311) (-, 378, -) sts.

Sizes 32 and 44" Only:

INCREASE ROW 5 (RS): K4, sm, *[k1-f/b, - (25, -, -) (12, -, -)] - (1, -, -) (2, -, -) time(s), [k1-f/b, k- (24, -, -) (11, -, -)] - (4, -, -) (3, -, -) time(s); repeat from * to marker, sm, k4— - (270, -, -) (343, -, -) sts.

Sizes 36 and 52" Only:

INCREASE ROW 5 (RS): K4, sm, k1-f/b, k- (-, 13, -) (-, -, 9), *k1-f/b, k- (-, 12, -) (-, -, 10); repeat from * to - (-, 14, -) (-, -, 10) sts before marker, k1-f/b, k- (-, 13, -) (-, -, 9), sm, k4— - (-, 290, -) (-, -, 390) sts.

All Sizes:

Purl 1 row, keeping first and last 4 sts in Garter st.

Sizes 28, 36, and 52" Only:

INCREASE ROW 6 (RS): K4, sm, k1-f/b, k29 (-, 14, -) (-, -, 10), *k1-f/b, k30

(-, 13, -) (-, -, 11); repeat from * to 30 (-, 15, -) (-, -, 11) sts before marker, k1-f/b, k29 (-, 14, -) (-, -, 10), sm, k4—262 (-, 310, -) (-, -, 422) sts.

Size 32" Only:

INCREASE ROW 6 (RS): K4, sm, k1-f/b, k26, *k1-f/b, k25; repeat from * to 27 sts before marker, k1-f/b, k27, sm, k4—280 sts.

Sizes 40, 44, and 48" Only:

INCREASE ROW 6 (RS): K4, sm, [k1-f/b, k- (-, -, 12) (14, 13, -)] - (-, -, 2) (2, 1, -) time(s), *k1-f/b, k- (-, -, 13) (14, 14, -), [k1-f/b, k- (-, -, 12) (13, 13, -)] - (-, -, 4) (1, 3, -) time(s); repeat from * to - (-, -, 13) (15, 14, -) sts before marker, k1-f/b, k- (-, -, 12) (14, 13, -), sm, k4— - (-, -, 334) (366, 404, -) sts.

All Sizes:

Work even in Stockinette stitch, keeping first and last 4 sts in Garter st, until piece measures 7 (7, 7½, 8) (8, 8, 8)" [18 (18, 19, 20.5) (20.5, 20.5, 20.5) cm] from the beginning, ending with a WS row.

JOIN YOKE

JOINING RND (RS): Knit, removing markers. Pm for beginning of rnd. Work even in St st (knit every rnd) until piece measures 8 (8½, 8½, 9) (9½, 10, 10½)" [20.5 (21.5, 21.5, 23) (24, 25.5, 26.5) cm] from the beginning.

DIVIDE BODY AND SLEEVES

DIVISION RND: K40 (44, 49, 53) (58, 63, 67) for left front, place next 51 (52, 57, 61) (67, 76, 77) sts onto waste yarn for left sleeve, using Backward Loop CO (see Special Techniques, page 168), CO 2 (3, 4, 5) (6, 6, 8) sts for underarm, pm for beginning of rnd, CO 2 (3, 4, 5) (6, 6, 8) sts for underarm, k80 (88, 98, 106) (116, 126, 134) for back, place next 51 (52, 57, 61) (67, 76, 77) sts onto waste yarn for right sleeve, CO 2 (3, 4, 5) (6, 6, 8) sts for underarm, pm for side, CO 2 (3, 4, 5) (6, 6, 8) sts for underarm, knit to beginning of rnd—168 (188, 212, 232) (256, 276, 300) sts remain.

BODY

Work in St st until piece measures 11½ (11½, 12, 11½) (12, 12, 12)" [29 (29, 30.5, 29) (30.5, 30.5, 30.5) cm] from underarm.

NEXT RND: Work to marker, place next 84 (94, 106, 116) (128, 138, 150) sts. Place remaining sts onto waste yarn for front.

NEXT ROW (WS): K4, pm, purl to last 4 sts, pm, k4.

Work 11 rows in St st, keeping first and last 4 sts in Garter st.

Knit 7 rows.

BO all sts.

With RS facing, return front sts to needle and rejoin yarn.

NEXT ROW (WS): K4, pm, purl to last 4 sts, pm, k4.

Work 7 rows in St st, keeping first and last 4 sts in Garter st.

Knit 7 rows.

BO all sts.

SLEEVES

Transfer sleeve sts to needle(s) in preferred style for small-circumference knitting in the rnd. Beginning at center of underarm, pick up and knit 2 (3, 4, 5) (6, 6, 8) sts from sts CO for underarm, knit across sts from yoke, pick up and knit 2 (3, 4, 5) (6, 6, 8) sts from sts CO for underarm—55 (58, 65, 71) (79, 88, 93) sts. Join for working in the rnd; pm for beginning of rnd.

Begin St st; work 3 rnds even.

SHAPE SLEEVE

DECREASE RND: K1, k2tog, knit to last 3 sts, ssk, k1—2 sts decreased.

Knit 2 rnds.

Repeat Decrease Rnd once more—51 (54, 61, 67) (75, 84, 89) sts remain.

Knit 2 rnds.

Work 7 rnds in Garter st (purl 1 rnd, knit 1 rnd).

BO all sts loosely purlwise.

FINISHING

Block as desired. Use tails to close gaps at underarms.

MARKET DAY BAG

The Market Day Bag is surprisingly versatile and sturdy. It's useful for trips to the farmers' market, the park, and the beach, or it can be used as a purse. The cotton and linen in the chosen yarn work together to create a durable fabric. Alternative materials can be denim yarn, raffia, pure linen—anything that lacks stretch and is a natural fiber.

FINISHED MEASUREMENTS
35" (89 cm) circumference; 20" (51.5 cm) height, with piece measured flat, not including the straps

YARN
Juniper Moon Farm Zooey [60% cotton, 40% linen; 284 yards (259 meters) / 100 grams]: 3 balls #8 All Spice

NEEDLES
One set of four or five double-pointed needles and one 16" (40 cm) circular needle size US 3 (3.25 mm)

One 16" (40 cm) circular needle size US 5 (3.75 mm)
Change needle size if necessary to obtain correct gauge.

NOTIONS
Stitch marker, removable stitch marker, tapestry needle

GAUGE
30 sts and 32 rows = 4" (10 cm) in St st, using smaller needles
22 sts and 28 rows = 4" (10 cm) in St st, using larger needle

STITCH PATTERN

MINIATURE LEAVES

(multiple of 6 sts; 4-rnd repeat)

RND 1: *K3, yo, sk2p, yo; repeat from * to end.

RND 2: Knit.

RND 3: *Yo, sk2p, yo, k3; repeat from * to end.

RND 4: Knit.

Repeat Rnds 1–4 for Miniature Leaves.

BAG

Using smaller double-pointed needles, CO 8 sts onto one dpn.

SET-UP ROW (RS): *K1-f/b; repeat from * to end—16 sts. Do not turn. Divide sts among 3 or 4 dpns and join for working in the rnd, being careful not to twist sts; pm for beginning of rnd.

RND 1: Knit.

RND 2: *K1, k1-f/b; repeat from * to end—24 sts.

RND 3: *K3, pm; repeat from * to end, omitting last pm (beginning-of-rnd marker is here).

SHAPE BOTTOM

NOTE: Change to smaller circular needle when necessary for number of sts on needles.

INCREASE RND: *K1-f/b, knit to marker, sm; repeat from * to end—8 sts increased.

Repeat Increase Rnd every other rnd 20 more times—192 sts (24 sts each section).

BODY

Continuing in St st (knit every rnd), work 2" (5 cm) even, removing all markers except beginning-of-rnd marker on first rnd.

Change to larger needle.

*Begin Miniature Leaves; work 4-rnd repeat 4 times.

Knit 7 rnds.

Repeat from * once more.

Change to smaller circular needle.

Begin circular Garter st (purl 1 rnd, knit 1 rnd); work 1¼" (3 cm) even, ending with a knit rnd.

SHAPE HANDLES

ROW 1 (RS): Knit 96, place the next 96 sts on waste yarn—96 sts remain.

ROW 2: Working on one handle only, knit.

ROW 3: [K1, ssk] twice, knit to last 6 sts, [k2tog, k1] twice—4 sts decreased.

ROW 4: Knit.

ROWS 5–10: Repeat Rows 3 and 4 three times—80 sts remain after Row 9.

ROW 11: [K1, ssk] 6 times, work to last 18 sts, [k2tog, k1] 6 times—12 sts decreased.

ROW 12: Knit.

ROWS 13–16: Repeat Rows 11 and 12 three times—32 sts remain after Row 15.

ROW 17: K1, ssk, knit to last 3 sts, k2tog, k1—2 sts decreased.

ROW 18: Knit.

ROWS 19–36: Repeat Rows 17 and 18 nine times—12 sts remain after Row 35. Place removable marker at end of Row 35.

Continue in flat Garter st (knit every row) until piece measures 19" (48.5 cm) from marker, slightly stretched.

BO all sts.

SECOND HANDLE

With RS facing, rejoin yarn to sts on hold for second handle. Knit 1 row.

Complete as for first handle, beginning with Row 2.

FINISHING

Using tapestry needle and CO tail, thread tail through CO sts and pull tight. Fasten off to inside. Block as desired. Tie handle ends together at top with an overhand knot. The handles will be stretchy, so retie whenever necessary.

LATE SUMMER SKIMMER SOCKS

You'll want to make dozens of these little no-show socks! They use a small amount of sock yarn, they're quick, and they can double as house slippers.

SIZES
Children's Large/Women's Small (Women's Medium, Women's Large/Men's Small, Men's Medium, Men's Large)

FINISHED MEASUREMENTS
6¾ (7½, 8, 8½, 9¼)" [17 (19, 20.5, 21.5, 23.5) cm] foot circumference, measured approximately 2½ (2¾, 2¾, 3, 3)" [6.5 (7, 7, 7.5, 7.5) cm] from tip of toe
7½ (8½, 9, 9½, 10)" [19 (21.5, 23, 24, 25.5) cm] foot length
NOTE: Total foot length should be approximately 1" (2.5 cm) less than wearer's foot length.

YARN
Koigu Painters Palette Premium Merino (KPPPM) [100% merino wool; 170 yards (155 meters) / 50 grams]: 1 (1, 1, 1, 2) skein(s) #620 (mostly orange)

NEEDLES
One set of five double-pointed needles size US 3 (3.25 mm)
One 16" circular needle size US 2 (2.75 mm)
Change needle size if necessary to obtain correct gauge.

NOTIONS
Stitch markers, waste yarn, crochet hook size US D-3 (3.25 mm)

GAUGE
28 sts and 36 rows = 4" (10 cm) in St st

STITCH PATTERN

1X1 RIB
(even number of sts; 1-rnd repeat)
ALL RNDS: *K1, p1; repeat from * to end.

PATTERN NOTES

These socks are worked from the toe up, beginning with a Provisional Cast-On at the toe. Once the toe shaping is complete, stitches are placed on hold for the instep while the sole is worked. Then the heel is shaped using double-wrap short rows. Finally, stitches are picked up for the ribbed foot band, and short-row shaping is used to shape the foot band at the heel.

For the best fit, the finished foot length of the sock should be 1" (2.5 cm) less than the wearer's total foot length.

TOE

Using waste yarn and Provisional CO (see Special Techniques, page 170), CO 8 (8, 10, 10, 10) sts. Change to working yarn.
Begin St st (purl 1 row, knit 1 row); work 4 rows even.
Rotate Toe so that Provisional CO is on top. Carefully unzip CO and place resulting 8 (8, 10, 10, 10) sts onto 2 empty dpns for the sole (the needle holding the original sts will be the instep)—16 (16, 20, 20, 20). Join for working in the rnd; pm for beginning of rnd.

SHAPE TOE

INCREASE RND: Needle 1: K1, M1R, knit to end of needle; Needle 2: Knit to last st, M1L, k1; Needle 3: K1, M1R, knit to last st, M1L, k1—4 sts increased.
Repeat Increase Rnd every other rnd 7 (8, 8, 9, 10) more times—48 (52, 56, 60, 64) sts; 12 (13, 14, 15, 16) sole sts each on Needles 1 and 2, and 24 (26, 28, 30, 32) instep sts on Needle 3.
Work even until piece measures 2½ (2¾, 3, 3¼, 3½)" [6.5 (7, 7.5, 8.5, 9) cm] from the tip of the toe.

SOLE

Separate Instep from Sole
NEXT RND: Needle 1: Knit; Needle 2: Knit to end, k2 from Needle 3; Needle 3: Knit to last 2 sts and place previous 20 (22, 24, 26, 28) sts onto waste yarn, slip last 2 sts from Needle 3 onto Needle 1, removing beginning-of-rnd marker—28 (30, 32, 34, 36) sts remain.
NEXT ROW (RS): Slip 1 wyib, knit to end.

NEXT ROW (WS): Slip 1 wyif, purl to end.
Work until piece measures 5 (5¾, 6¼, 6½, 7)" [12.5 (14.5, 16, 16.5, 18) cm] from tip of Toe, or to 2½ (2¾, 2¾, 3, 3)" [6.5 (7, 7, 7.5, 7.5) cm] less than desired length to back of heel, ending with a WS row.

SHORT-ROW HEEL

SHORT ROW 1 (RS): K27 (29, 31, 33, 35) sts, w&t.
SHORT ROW 2 (WS): P26 (28, 30, 32, 34) sts, w&t.
SHORT ROW 3: Knit to 1 st before wrapped st from previous RS row, w&t.
SHORT ROW 4: Purl to 1 st before wrapped st from previous WS row, w&t.
Repeat Short Rows 3 and 4 ten (11, 11, 12, 13) more times—6 (6, 8, 8, 8) sts remain between wrapped sts at center of heel.
SHORT ROW 5 (RS): Knit to first wrapped st from previous RS row, knit wrapped st, w&t.
SHORT ROW 6 (WS): Purl to first wrapped st from previous WS row, purl wrapped st, w&t.
SHORT ROW 7: Knit to double-wrapped st, knit wrapped st, w&t.
SHORT ROW 8: Purl to double-wrapped st, purl wrapped st, w&t.
Repeat Short Rows 7 and 8 until you have wrapped the last st on

either side of the heel. Pm at center of heel sts.

FOOT BAND

Place live heel sts and center marker onto smaller circular needle. Place held toe sts onto spare dpn.

Using circular needle holding heel sts, pm, pick up and knit an even number of sts along side edge of sole to held toe sts, knit held toe sts onto circular needle, pick up and knit the same number of sts along second side edge of sole heel, pm, knit to marker at center of heel (this is new beginning-of-rnd marker).

Begin 1x1 Rib; work 1 rnd.

SHAPE BACK OF HEEL

SHORT ROW 1 (RS): Work to 1 st before marker, w&t.

SHORT ROW 2 (WS): Work to beginning-of-rnd marker, sm, work to 1 st before next marker, w&t.

SHORT ROW 3: Work to wrapped st from previous RS row, work wrap together with wrapped st, work 3 sts, w&t.

SHORT ROW 4: Work to wrapped st from previous WS row, work wrap together with wrapped st, work 3 sts, w&t.

SHORT ROW 5: Work to beginning-of-rnd marker.

Work 5 rnds even, working wraps together with wrapped sts as you come to them.

BO all sts in pattern.

FINISHING

Block as desired.

TASSEL TANK

Everyone has a fashionable family member or friend who would love a knit tank like this. You can finish the ties in the back with whatever you like: tassels as shown, little pom-poms for someone young at heart, or even simple knots.

FINISHED MEASUREMENTS
28 (32, 36, 40) (44, 48, 52, 56)" [71 (81.5, 91.5, 101.5) (112, 122, 132, 142) cm] chest circumference

YARN
Berroco Remix [30% nylon, 27% cotton, 24% acrylic, 10% silk, 9% linen; 216 yards (198 meters) / 100 grams]: 2 (2, 3, 3) (3, 3, 4, 4) skeins #3922 Buttercup

NEEDLES
One 24" (60 cm) long or longer circular needle size US 8 (5 mm)
One pair double-pointed needles size US 8 (5 mm) (optional; for edging and I-cords)

NOTE: If you work the knit edging and I-cord, choose the same size needles for both, but if your gauge seems too loose, go down a needle size.
Change needle size if necessary to obtain correct gauge.

NOTIONS
Stitch markers, waste yarn, 1½" (4 mm) tassel maker (optional), crochet hook size US I-9 (5.5 mm) (optional)

GAUGE
16 sts and 24 rnds = 4" (10 cm) in St st

STITCH PATTERN

SHADOW RIB

(multiple of 3 sts; 2-rnd repeat)
RND 1: P1, *k1-tbl, p2; repeat from * to last 2 sts, k1-tbl, k1.
RND 2: Purl.
Repeat Rnds 1 and 2 for Shadow Rib.

PATTERN NOTES

This piece is worked from the bottom to the armholes in one piece, then front and back are worked separately to the end. You may work either a crochet or a knit edging at the top of the front and back. You may work an optional crochet edging along the armholes, or leave them unfinished. You may work either crochet chain or I-cord ties.

BODY

CO 120 (138, 150, 168) (186, 192, 216, 234) sts. Join for working in the rnd, begin careful not to twist sts; pm for beginning of rnd.
Begin Shadow Rib; work even for 2" (5 cm), ending with Rnd 1 of pattern; pm after 60 (69, 75, 84) (93, 99, 108, 117) sts.
Change to St st (knit every rnd).

SHAPE BODY

DECREASE RND: [Decrease 1 st randomly between markers (working decrease as k2tog)] twice—1 st decreased each for front and back.
Repeat Decrease Rnd every 6 rnds 3 (4, 2, 3) (4, 2, 3, 4) more times—112 (128, 144, 160) (176, 192, 208, 224) sts remain.
Work even until piece measures 12 (12, 11¾, 11½) (11¼, 12, 11½, 12)" [30.5 (30.5, 30, 29) (28.5, 30.5, 29, 30.5) cm] from the beginning.
DIVISION RND: Work 56 (64, 72, 80) (88, 96, 104, 112) sts for front, place next 56 (64, 72, 80) (88, 96, 104, 112) sts onto waste yarn for back.

FRONT

Working on front sts only, purl 1 row.
Continue in St st (knit 1 row, purl 1 row) for remainder of piece.

SHAPE ARMHOLES

DECREASE ROW: Work 1 st as established, ssk (ssp if working on the WS), work to last 3 sts, k2tog (p2tog if working on the WS), work 1 st—2 sts decreased.
Repeat Decrease Row every 3 rows 8 (6, 5, 5) (3, 3, 2, 0) times, then every 2 rows 5 (9, 12, 14) (18, 20, 23, 27) times—28 (32, 36, 40) (44, 48, 52, 56) sts remain.
Work even if necessary until armholes measure 6½ (7, 7½, 8) (8½, 9, 9½, 10)" [16.5 (18, 19, 20.5) (21.5, 23, 24, 25.5) cm], ending with a WS row.
BO all sts.

BACK

With RS facing, rejoin yarn to back sts.
Work 2 rows even in St st.

SHAPE BACK

DECREASE ROW 1 (RS): [K1, ssk] 3 times, knit to last 9 sts, [k2tog, k1] 3 times—6 sts decreased.
Repeat Decrease Row 1 every RS row 0 (2, 2, 2) (2, 2, 2, 4) times—50 (46, 54, 62) (70, 78, 86, 82) sts remain.
DECREASE ROW 2 (RS): [K1, ssk] twice, knit to last 6 sts, [k2tog, k1] twice—4 sts decreased.
Repeat Decrease Row 1 every RS row 9 (8, 10, 12) (14, 16, 18, 17) more times—10 sts remain.
BO all sts.

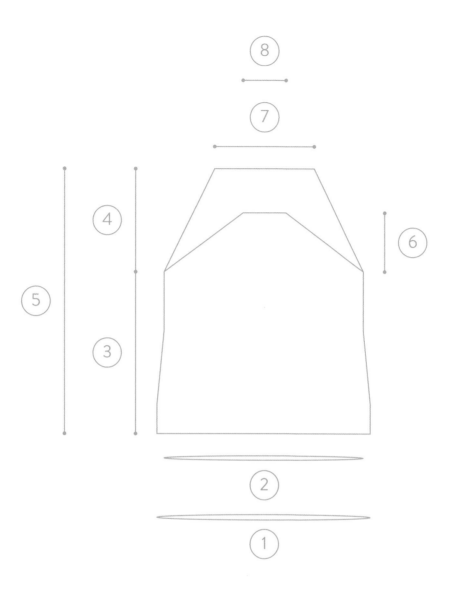

1   30 (34½, 37½, 42) (46½, 49½, 54, 58½)"
    76 (87.5, 95.5, 106.5) (118, 125.5, 137, 148.5) cm

2   28 (32, 36, 40) (44, 48, 52, 56)"
    71 (81.5, 91.5, 101.5) (112, 122, 132, 142) cm

3   12 (12, 11¾, 11½) (11¼, 12, 11½, 12)"
    30.5 (30.5, 30, 29) (28.5, 30.5, 29, 30.5) cm

4   6½ (7, 7½, 8) (8½, 9, 9½, 10)"
    16.5 (18, 19, 20.5) (21.5, 23, 24, 25.5) cm

5   18½ (19, 19¼, 19½) (19¾, 21, 21, 22)"
    47 (48.5, 49, 49.5) (50, 53.5, 53.5, 56) cm

6   ------
    ------

7   7 (8, 9, 10) (11, 12, 13, 14)"
    18 (20.5, 23, 25.5) (28, 30.5, 33, 35.5) cm

8   2½"
    6.5 cm

FINISHING

FRONT TOP EDGING

CROCHET OPTION

With RS of front facing, using crochet hook, work 1 row of single crochet (see Special Techniques, page 171) along top edge of front. Fasten off.

KNIT OPTION

With RS of front facing, using circular needle, pick up and knit 1 st in each BO st along top of front. BO all sts purlwise.

BACK TOP EDGING

CROCHET OPTION

With RS of back facing, using crochet hook, work 1 row of single crochet along top edge of back to center back, crochet chain 4 (see Special Techniques, page 171), join with a slip st to edge, work single crochet to end. Fasten off.

KNIT OPTION

With RS of front facing, using dpn, pick up and knit 1 st in each BO st along top of back to center back, [yo] twice, pick up and knit 1 st in each BO st to end. BO all sts purlwise, working k1, p1 into yo as you BO.

RIGHT ARMHOLE CROCHET EDGING AND TIE OPTIONS

With RS of back facing, using crochet hook and beginning at top right edge of back armhole, work Crab Stitch (see Special Techniques, page 168) along armhole edge to top of right front armhole, then work crochet chain for 27" (68.5 cm) or to desired length; fasten off. Chain must be long enough to cross over shoulder to center back, with enough extra length to tie in a bow with the opposite tie.

LEFT ARMHOLE CROCHET EDGING AND TIE OPTIONS

Work crochet edging and chain the same length as for right tie. With RS of front facing, fasten chain with slip st to top left edge of front armhole, work Crab Stitch along armhole edge to top of left back armhole, fasten off.

I-CORD TIES OPTIONS

With RS of front facing, using dpns, pick up and knit 3 sts at top corner of right armhole edge. Work 3-st I-cord (see Special Techniques, page 168) for 27" (68.5 cm) or to desired length. I-cord must be long enough to cross over shoulder to center back, with enough extra length to tie a bow with the opposite tie. BO all sts. Work a second tie at opposite end of front.

TASSELS (OPTIONAL)

Using tassel maker (or following instructions in Special Techniques, page 171), make two 1½" (4 cm) tassels. Attach one tassel to end of each tie.

Block as desired.

Autumn is a magical time

when the leaves on the trees turn into a riot of wild colors, and the once-green grass turns yellow. All of a sudden, it's time for a harvest: grapes to be made into wine and juice, pumpkins for carving, and apples for delicious-smelling pies and cider. We gather to be thankful for our blessings, we begin readying for the upcoming winter holidays, and we knit: Knitting time is all the time during autumn. We love to knit and wear scarves, warm caps, cozy mittens, and holiday sweaters.

"By late autumn the yard would grow thick with fallen leaves, causing the landlady to heave many deep sighs." —TAKASHI HIRAIDE

"Every leaf speaks bliss to me, / Fluttering from the autumn tree." —EMILY BRONTË

"Delicious autumn! My very soul is wedded to it, and if I were a bird I would fly about the earth seeking the successive autumns." —GEORGE ELIOT

"It was a beautiful bright autumn day, with air like cider and a sky so blue you could drown in it." —DIANA GABALDON

"Fall has always been my favorite season. The time when everything bursts with its last beauty, as if nature had been saving up all year for the grand finale." —LAUREN DESTEFANO

"And all the lives we ever lived and all the lives to be / Are full of trees and changing leaves." —VIRGINIA WOOLF

STAIRCASE COWL

....

Some of my favorite projects are those that look intricate but are actually not, so don't be fooled by the mosaic-knitting staircase-like motif in this two-color cowl. It begins with some ribbing in the round, and then the second color is introduced. For each color, just two rounds are worked while the other one waits inside. What's more, there are hardly any ends to weave in when the project is complete!

FINISHED MEASUREMENTS
22" (56 cm) circumference x 11¼" (28.5 cm) length

YARN
Ewe Ewe Yarns Wooly Worsted [100% superwash merino; 95 yards (87 meters) / 50 grams]: 2 skeins each #92 Wheat (A) and #80 Indigo (B)
NOTE: The sample used almost all of 2 skeins of A; you may wish to purchase an additional skein to ensure you do not run out.

NEEDLES
One 16" (40 cm) long circular needle size US 8 (5 mm)

Change needle size if necessary to obtain correct gauge.

NOTIONS
Stitch marker

GAUGE
24 sts and 22 rnds = 4" (10 cm) in Staircase Slip Stitch

STITCH PATTERNS

3X3 RIB
(multiple of 6 sts; 1-rnd repeat)
ALL RNDS: *K3, p3; repeat from * to end.

PATTERN NOTES

You may work Staircase Slip Stitch from text or chart.
Slip all sts purlwise with yarn in back.

STAIRCASE SLIP STITCH

(multiple of 6 sts; 12-rnd repeat)

RNDS 1 AND 2: With B, *slip 2, k4; repeat from * to end.

RNDS 3 AND 4: With A, *k4, slip 2; repeat from * to end.

RNDS 5 AND 6: With B, k2, slip 2, *k4, slip 2; repeat from * to last 2 sts, k2.

RNDS 7 AND 8: With A, repeat Rnds 1 and 2.

RNDS 9 AND 10: With B, repeat Rnds 3 and 4.

RNDS 11 AND 12: With A, repeat Rnds 5 and 6.

Repeat Rnds 1–12 for Staircase Slip Stitch.

COWL

Using A, CO 132 sts. Join for working in the rnd, being careful not to twist sts; pm for beginning of rnd.

Begin 3x3 Rib; work even for 1" (2.5 cm).

Change to Staircase Slip Stitch; work even until piece measures 10¼" (26 cm) from the beginning, ending with Rnd 2, 6, or 10 of pattern.

Change to A and 3x3 Rib; work even for 1" (2.5 cm).

BO all sts in pattern.

FINISHING

Block as desired.

Knit

Slip 1 wyib

A

B

Staircase Slip Stitch

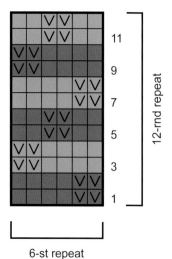

12-rnd repeat

6-st repeat

LAZY DAY SWEATER

Autumn, with the falling leaves and changing colors, brings on feelings of spending lazy days exploring and goofing off. This youth-size pattern is unisex and can be knit by beginners and experts alike. Does your recipient have a favorite football team? Imagine knitting in the team colors or placing contrasting stripes on one of the sleeves.

SIZES
12 months (2, 4, 6) (8, 10, 12) years

FINISHED MEASUREMENTS
23½ (25¼, 26¾, 28¼) (30½, 31¼, 33½)" [59.5 (64, 68, 72) (77.5, 79.5, 85) cm] chest

YARN
Blue Sky Fibers Woolstok [100% fine highland wool; 123 yards (112 meters) / 50 grams]: 4 (4, 5, 5) (6, 7, 8) hanks #1311 Rusted Roof

NEEDLES
One set of four or five double-pointed needles and one 24"

(60 cm) long or longer circular needle size US 6 (4.25 mm) Change needle size if necessary to obtain correct gauge.

NOTIONS
Stitch markers, waste yarn

GAUGE
21 sts and 24 rnds = 4" (10 cm) in St st

STITCH PATTERNS

CIRCULAR 5X2 RIB
(multiple of 7 sts; 1-rnd repeat)
ALL RNDS: *K5, p2; repeat from * to end.

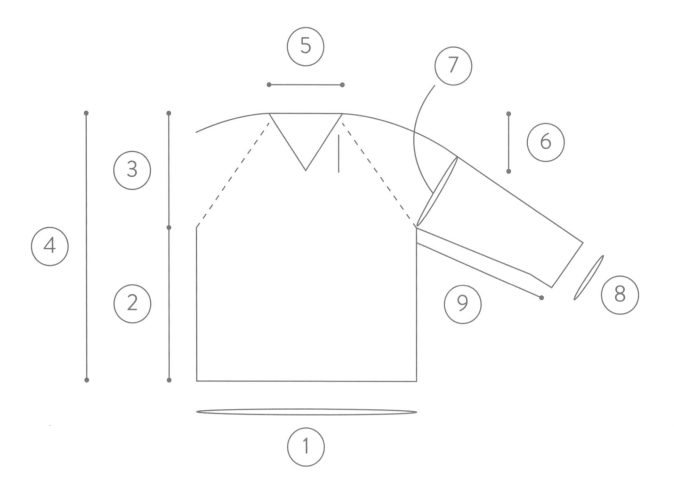

1   23½ (25¼, 26¾, 28¼) (30½, 31¼, 33½)"
59.5 (64, 68, 72) (77.5, 79.5, 85) cm

2   7¾ (9¼, 9¾, 10½) (10½, 12¼, 13½)"
19.5 (23.5, 25, 26.5) (26.5, 31, 34.5) cm

3   5¾ (6¼, 6¼, 7) (7½, 7¾, 8½)"
14.5 (16, 16, 18) (19, 19.5, 21.5) cm

4   13½ (15½, 16, 17½) (18, 20, 22)"
34.5 (39.5, 40.5, 44.5) (45.5, 51, 56) cm

5   3¾ (3¾, 4¼, 4¼) (4½, 4½, 5)"
9.5 (9.5, 11, 11) (11.5, 11.5, 12.5) cm

6   3¼ (3¼, 4, 4) (4¾, 4¾, 5¼)"
8.5 (8.5, 10, 10) (12, 12, 13.5) cm

7   8¾ (9½, 10, 10¾) (11, 11½, 12¼)"
22 (24, 25.5, 27.5) (28, 29, 31) cm

8   6¾ (6¾, 6¾, 8½) (8½, 8½, 8½)"
17 (17, 17, 21.5) (21.5, 21.5, 21.5) cm

9   7½ (9½, 10½, 11½) (12½, 13½, 15)"
19 (24, 26.5, 29) (32, 34.5, 38) cm

FLAT 5X2 RIB

(multiple of 7 sts + 2; 2-row repeat)

ROW 1 (WS): K2, *p5, k2; repeat from * to end.

ROW 2: P2, *k5, p2; repeat from * to end.

Repeat Rows 1 and 2 for Flat 5x2 Rib.

PATTERN NOTES

This sweater is worked in one piece from the top down to the underarms, then body and sleeves are worked separately in the round to the bottom edge.

YOKE

Using circular needle, CO 3 sts for front, pm, 4 (4, 4, 4) (2, 2, 2) sts for sleeve, pm, 20 (20, 22, 22) (24, 24, 26) sts for back, pm, 4 (4, 4, 4) (2, 2, 2) sts for sleeve, pm, 2 sts for front—34 (34, 36, 36) (34, 34, 36) sts.

SHAPE RAGLAN AND NECK

YOKE INCREASE ROW (RS): [Knit to 1 st before marker, k1-f/b, sm, k1-f/b] 4 times, knit to end—8 sts increased.

Purl 1 row.

NECK AND YOKE INCREASE ROW (RS): K1-f/b, [knit to 1 st before marker, k1-f/b, sm, k1-f/b] 4 times, knit to

last st, k1-f/b—10 sts increased.

Purl 1 row.

Repeat last 4 rows 4 (4, 5, 5) (6, 6, 7) more times—124 (124, 144, 144) (160, 160, 180) sts.

JOIN NECK

JOINING ROW (RS): [Knit to 1 st before marker, k1-f/b] 4 times, knit to end, CO 2 sts, pm for new beginning of rnd, CO 2 sts— 136 (136, 156, 156) (172, 172, 192) sts. Join for working in the rnd. Knit to end.

YOKE INCREASE RND: [Knit to 1 st before marker, k1-f/b, sm, k1-f/b] 4 times, knit to end—8 sts increased.

Knit 1 rnd.

Repeat last 2 rnds 4 (6, 4, 6) (6, 7, 7) more times—176 (192, 196, 212) (228, 236, 256) sts.

DIVIDE FOR BODY AND SLEEVES

DIVISION RND: Knit to marker, place next 36 (40, 40, 44) (46, 48, 52) sts onto waste yarn for left sleeve (removing markers), CO 5 (5, 6, 6) (6, 6, 6) sts for underarm, pm for new beginning of rnd, CO 5 (5, 6, 6) (6, 6, 6) sts, knit to next marker, place next 36 (40, 40, 44) (46, 48, 52) sts onto waste yarn for right sleeve (removing markers), CO 5 (5, 6, 6) (6, 6, 6) sts for underarm, pm,

CO 5 (5, 6, 6) (6, 6, 6) sts, knit to end—124 (132, 140, 148) (160, 164, 176) sts.

Begin St st (knit every rnd); work even until piece measures 5¾ (6¾, 7¼, 8) (7¾, 9½, 10¾)" [14.5 (17, 18.5, 20.5) (19.5, 24, 27.5) cm] from underarm, increasing 2 (1, 0, 0) (1, 4, 0) st(s) or decreasing 0 (0, 0, 1) (0, 0, 1) st(s) evenly on last rnd—126 (133, 140, 147) (161, 168, 175) sts.

Begin Circular 5x2 Rib; work even for 2 (2½, 2½, 2½) (2¾, 2¾, 2¾)" [5 (6.5, 6.5, 6.5) (7, 7, 7) cm]. BO all sts loosely in pattern.

SLEEVES

Transfer sleeve sts to dpns. Beginning at center of underarm, pick up and knit 5 (5, 6, 6) (6, 6, 6) sts from sts CO for underarm, knit across sts from yoke, pick up and knit 5 (5, 6, 6) (6, 6, 6) sts from sts CO for underarm—46 (50, 52, 56) (58, 50, 64) sts. Join for working in the rnd; pm for beginning of rnd.

Begin St st; work 6 rnds even.

SHAPE SLEEVE

DECREASE RND: K1, k2tog, knit to last 3 sts, ssk, k1—2 sts decreased.

Repeat Decrease Rnd every 4 (5, 6, 6) (7, 8, 7) rnds 4 (6, 7, 5) (6, 7, 9) more times—36 (36, 36, 44)

(44, 44, 44) sts remain.
Work even until piece measures
6½ (8, 9, 10) (11, 11½, 13)" from
underarm, decreasing 1 (1, 1, 2)
(2, 2, 2) st(s) before and/or after
beginning-of-rnd marker on last
rnd—35 (35, 35, 42) (42, 42, 42)
sts.
Change to Circular 5x2 Rib; work
even for 1 (1½, 1½, 1½) (1½, 2, 2)"
[2.5 (4, 4, 4) (4, 5, 5) cm].
BO all sts in pattern.

COLLAR

With RS facing, using circular
needle and beginning at bottom
center of front neck, pick up and
knit 19 (19, 24, 24) (29, 29, 32) sts
along right front neck edge, 27
(27, 31, 31) (28, 28, 29) sts along
sleeve and back CO edge, then 19
(19, 24, 24) (29, 29, 32) sts along
left front neck edge—65 (65, 79,
79) (86, 86, 93) sts. Do not join.
Begin Flat 5x2 Rib; work 3 rows
even.

SHAPE COLLAR

NOTE: Collar is shaped using short
rows (see Special Techniques,
page 171).
SHORT ROW 1 (RS): Work to last
5 sts, w&t.
SHORT ROW 2 (WS): Work to last
5 sts, w&t.

SHORT ROW 3: Work to 5 sts before
wrapped st from previous RS row,
w&t.
SHORT ROW 4: Work to 5 sts before
wrapped st from previous WS
row, w&t.
SHORT ROWS 5–8: Repeat Short
Rows 3 and 4 twice.
SHORT ROW 9: Work to end,
working wraps together with
wrapped sts as you come to them.

Work 8 rows even, working wraps
together with wrapped sts as you
come to them on first row.
BO all sts in pattern.

FINISHING

Block as desired.

FOXY PONCHO

....

Depending upon the colors you select, you can unleash your imagination and create another favorite woodland animal like a squirrel, a rabbit (use the ears in the Bunny Ears Hat on page 31 as a model), a raccoon, a bear . . . a skunk! Let your creativity run wild with this one.

SIZES
2–3 (4–5, 6–8) years

FINISHED MEASUREMENTS
37½ (40, 42)" [95.5 (101.5, 106.5) cm] bottom circumference

YARN
Blue Sky Fibers Woolstok [100% fine highland wool; 123 yards (112 meters) / 50 grams]: 3 (4, 5) skeins #1323 Ember Glow (MC); 1 skein each #1303 Highland Fleece (A) and #1313 Dark Chocolate (B)

NEEDLES
One 24" (60 cm) long or longer circular needle and one pair straight needles size US 6 (4 mm)

Change needle size if necessary to obtain correct gauge.

NOTIONS
Stitch markers (including one in unique color or style for beginning of rnd); crochet hook size US G-6 (4 mm) (optional)

GAUGE
20 sts and 24 rows = 4" (10 cm) in St st

STITCH PATTERN

2X2 RIB
(multiple of 4 sts; 1-rnd repeat)
ALL RNDS: *K2, p2; repeat from * to end.

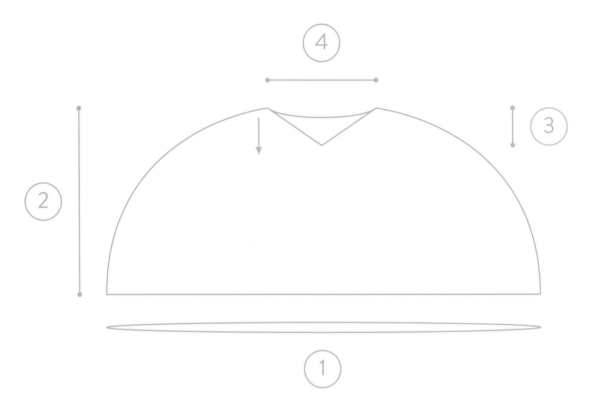

1	37½ (40, 42)" 95 1/2 (101 1/2, 106 1/2) cm
2	10 (11½, 12½)" 25 1/2 (29, 32) cm
3	2 (2¼, 2¾)" 5 (5 1/2, 7) cm
4	6 (6½, 7¼)" 54 (56, 64) cm

This poncho is worked in rows from the top to the end of the neck shaping, then joined and worked in the round to the bottom edge. The hood is picked up and worked to the top, then grafted or joined using your choice of Kitchener stitch or Three-Needle Bind-Off. Each ear is worked in two pieces that are crocheted or sewn together, then sewn to the hood.

PONCHO

Using MC, CO 2 sts, pm in unique color or style for left shoulder, CO 10 (10, 12) sts, pm for back, CO 30 (32, 36) sts, pm for right shoulder, CO 10 (10, 12) sts, pm for right front, CO 2 sts—54 (56, 64) sts. Do not join.
Purl 1 row.

SHAPE SHOULDERS AND NECK

SHOULDER INCREASE ROW (RS): [Knit to 1 st before marker, k1-f/b, sm, k1-f/b] 4 times, knit to end—8 sts increased.
Purl 1 row.
Repeat Shoulder Increase Row once more—70 (72, 80) sts.
Purl 1 row.

SHOULDER AND NECK INCREASE ROW (RS): K1-f/b, [knit to 1 st before marker, k1-f/b, sm, k1-f/b] 4 times, knit to last st, k1-f/b—10 sts increased.
Repeat Shoulder and Neck Increase Row every other row 2 (3, 4) more times—100 (112, 130) sts.
Purl 1 row.
Repeat Shoulder Increase Row once more—108 (120, 138) sts. Do not turn; join for working in the rnd; knit to left shoulder marker (this will now be beginning-of-rnd marker).
Knit 1 rnd.

BODY INCREASE RND: [K1-f/b, knit to 1 st before marker, k1-f/b, sm] 4 times—8 sts increased.

Continuing in St st (knit every rnd), repeat Body Increase Rnd every other rnd 9 (9, 8) more times—188 (200, 210) sts.

Work even (removing all markers on first rnd except beginning-of-rnd marker) until piece measures 9 (10½, 11½)" [23 (26.5, 29) cm] from back neck edge, increasing 0 (0, 2) sts evenly on last rnd—156 (200, 212) sts.

Change to 2x2 Rib; work even for 1" (2.5 cm).

BO all sts loosely.

HOOD

With RS facing, using circular needle and MC, and beginning at base of front neck, pick up and knit 1 st in each row along right front neck edge, 1 st for every st along CO edge to left front, and 1 st in every row along left front neck edge to center, ending with an even number of sts. Do not join.

Begin St st; work even until piece measures 10 (10½, 12)" [25.5 (26.5, 30.5) cm] from pick-up row, ending with a RS row. Cut yarn, leaving a tail 4 times the width of the piece.

Divide sts in half onto two ends of circular needle. Using Kitchener st or Three-Needle BO (see Special Techniques, pages 169 and 172), graft or join sts.

FINISHING

HOOD EDGING

With RS facing, using circular needle and A, and beginning at center top of hood, pick up and knit approximately 3 sts for every 4 rows around entire neck opening. Join for working in the rnd; pm for beginning of rnd. Purl 1 rnd.

Change to B; work 7 rnds in Garter st (knit 1 rnd, purl 1 rnd). BO all sts knitwise.

EARS (MAKE 2 IN MC AND 2 IN A)

Using straight needles, CO 15 sts. Begin St st (knit 1 row, purl 1 row), beginning with a RS row; work 6 rows even.

SHAPE EAR

SET-UP ROW (RS): K5, ssk, pm, k1, k2tog, knit to end—13 sts remain. Work 3 rows even.

DECREASE ROW (RS): Knit to 2 sts before marker, ssk, sm, k1, k2tog, knit to end—2 sts decreased.

Repeat Decrease Row every RS row 4 more times—3 sts remain.

NEXT ROW (WS): Sp2p—1 st remains. Fasten off.

Weave in all ear ends except MC CO tail.

With WS of one MC and one A ear piece together, using crochet hook or tapestry needle and B, single crochet or whipstitch pieces together along outside edges, leaving bottom edges open. Repeat for second ear. Attach ears to head as desired (see photos), sewing through both bottom layers of ears while sewing in place.

Block as desired.

FELT BALL FALL GARLAND

Actually, this project isn't limited to the fall season. You could make this felt ball garland in a color or colors to embrace whatever your heart wants. A garland like this can be made into a mobile and given to a young couple for hanging over a baby crib, hung as a simple room divider—you can also make a series of balls of different sizes and re-create a hanging solar system as a fun project for school-age kids.

FINISHED MEASUREMENTS
Approximately 2½ yards (2.25 m) long (for one garland)

MATERIALS
EcoSoft Wool Roving [100% wool; 1 ounce (28.5 grams)]: 1 ounce (28.5 grams) each Slate, Sunflower, Sweet Corn, Flame, and Natural
NOTE: One ounce will yield approximately 10 balls.
Aunt Lydia's Crochet Thread Classic 10 [100% mercerized cotton; 350 yards (320 meters)]: 1 spool #21 Linen

NOTIONS
Digital kitchen scale, sharp needle with large eye, small washers or circular stitch markers (2 for each garland)

PATTERN NOTE
If your kitchen scale doesn't measure in .01 ounce (.025 gram) increments, measure the roving in the smallest increment possible, then divide as necessary so that each division will equal approximately .01 ounces (.025 grams).

FELT BALLS
NOTE: Follow instructions on page 151 for making felt balls.
Make six or eight 1" (2.5 cm) felt balls in each color (three or four per garland), using .01 ounces (.025 grams) of roving each. Allow to dry thoroughly.

GARLAND
Measure out a length of thread approximately 6" (15 cm) longer than intended garland. Make a knot approximately 6" (15 cm) before tail end (not needle end).

Thread needle with thread and push through center of first ball. Slide ball down to knot. Make another knot right after the felt ball to hold it in place.

Make a knot for next ball approximately 4" (10 cm) or desired distance from first ball. Thread needle through center of next felt ball. Slide ball down to needle and make a knot close to other side of ball.

Continue adding balls in this manner until you have threaded the number of balls you want on this garland, making a final knot after last ball. Remove needle and tie a washer to end of thread. Tie a second washer to opposite end of thread.

TIP: If the crochet thread is getting tangled, place the balls on a shorter piece, then tie on a new length of thread to extend the length. Tuck the knot into a felt ball to hide it.

FAMILY OF STRIPED MITTENS

These multisize mittens will fit virtually any friend or family member. Choose the coziest of woolen yarns for the most warmth—and remember there's a folded-in hemmed edge that will reveal a contrast color at the wrist for a little bit of whimsy and extra warmth.

SIZES
4–6 years (6–8 years, 8 years/ Women's Small, Women's Medium) (Women's Large/Men's Small, Men's Medium, Men's Large)

FINISHED MEASUREMENTS
6 (6¼, 7, 7¼) (7¾, 8¼, 9)" [15 (16, 18, 18.5) (19.5, 21, 23) cm] hand circumference

YARN
Morehouse Farm 2-Ply [100% merino wool; 225 yards (205 meters) / 2 ounces (57 grams)]
Striped Mittens: 1 skein each A, B, and C (for cuff lining)
Shown in:
Women's Medium: Oatmeal (A), Natural White (B), and Henna (C)
Men's Medium: Oatmeal (A), Navy (B), and Henna (C)
NOTE: You may use a small amount of sport-weight yarn from your stash for C.
Solid Mittens: 1 skein each A and C (for cuff lining)
Shown in:
6–8 years: Oatmeal (A) and Navy (C)
NOTE: You may use a small amount of sport-weight yarn from your stash for C.

NEEDLES
Needle(s) in preferred style for small-circumference knitting in the rnd, size US 4 (3.5 mm)
Change needle size if necessary to obtain correct gauge.

NOTIONS

Stitch markers (including one in unique color or style for beginning of rnd), waste yarn

GAUGE

24 sts and 34 rnds = 4" (10 cm) in St st

STITCH PATTERN

STRIPE PATTERN

Working in St st (knit every rnd), *work 4 rnds in A, then 2 rnds in B; repeat from * throughout.

PATTERN NOTE

You may either work in a solid color or stripes. If working stripes, do not cut yarn when changing colors; carry color not in use up WS of piece. To avoid color change jog at beginning of rnd, slip first st of rnd on second rnd of new color.

MITTENS (BOTH ALIKE)

CUFF LINING

Using C, CO 33 (36, 39, 42) (45, 47, 51) sts. Join for working in the rnd, being careful not to twist sts; pm in unique color or style for beginning of rnd.
Knit 8 rnds.
Purl 1 rnd (turning rnd).

CUFF

Change to A.
Begin St st (knit every rnd).
Working in Stripe Pattern or in single color as desired, work even until piece measures 2¼ (2½, 2½, 2¾) (2¾, 3, 3)" [5.5 (6.5, 6.5, 7) (7, 7.5, 7.5) cm] from turning rnd.
NEXT RND: Knit, increasing 3 (2, 3, 2) (1, 3, 3) st(s) evenly—36 (38, 42, 44) (46, 50, 54) sts.
Knit 1 rnd.

SHAPE THUMB GUSSET

SET-UP RND: K18 (19, 21, 22) (23, 25, 27), pm, M1L, pm, knit to end—37 (39, 43, 45) (47, 51, 55) sts; 1 st between gusset markers.
INCREASE RND: Knit to marker, sm, M1L, knit to marker, M1R, sm, knit to end—2 sts increased.
Repeat Increase Rnd every 3 rnds 4 (4, 4, 6) (6, 8, 7) times, then every 4 rnds 1 (1, 1, 0) (1, 0, 1) time(s)—49 (51, 55, 59) (63, 69, 73) sts; 13 (13, 13, 15) (17, 19, 19) sts between gusset markers.
NEXT RND: Knit to marker, remove marker, k13 (13, 13, 15) (17, 19, 19) and place these sts on waste yarn for thumb, remove marker, knit to end—36 (38, 42, 44) (46, 50, 54) sts remain.

HAND

Work even until piece measures 3½ (4, 4½, 5) (5½, 6, 6½)" [9 (10, 11.5, 12.5) (14, 15, 16.5) cm] from base of thumb.
NEXT RND: Knit, decreasing 0 (2, 2, 0) (2, 2, 2) sts evenly—36 (36, 40, 44) (44, 48, 52) sts remain.

SHAPE MITTEN TOP

DECREASE RND 1: *K7 (7, 8, 9) (9, 10, 11), k2tog, pm; repeat from * to end, omitting final pm (beginning of rnd marker is here)—32 (32, 36, 40) (40, 44, 48) sts remain.
Knit 1 rnd.
DECREASE RND 2: *Knit to 2 sts before marker, k2tog, sm; repeat from * to end—2 sts remain.
Repeat Decrease Rnd 2 every other rnd 0 (0, 1, 2) (4, 3, 4) more time(s), then every rnd 6 (6, 6, 6) (4, 6, 6) times—4 sts remain.
Cut yarn, leaving a long tail.
Thread tail through remaining sts, pull tight, and fasten off.

THUMB

Return held gusset sts to needle(s); rejoin yarn (matching Stripe Pattern if appropriate).
Pick up and knit 1 st in gap, knit to end—14 (14, 14, 16) (18, 20, 20) sts. Join for working in the rnd; pm for beginning of rnd.

Work in St st until piece measures 1 (1¼, 1¼, 1½) (1¾, 2, 2)" [2.5 (3, 3, 4) (4.5, 5, 5) cm] from pick-up rnd.

SHAPE THUMB TOP

RND 1: [K2tog, k3 (3, 3, 3) (4, 5, 5)] twice, k2tog, knit to end—11 (11, 11, 13) (15, 17, 17) sts remain.

RND 2: Knit.

RND 3: [K2tog, k2 (2, 2, 2) (3, 4, 4)] twice, k2tog, knit to end—8 (8, 8, 10) (12, 14, 14) sts remain.

RND 4: Knit.

RND 5: [K2tog, k1 (1, 1, 1) (2, 3, 3)] twice, k2tog, knit to end—5 (5, 5, 7) (9, 11, 11) sts remain.

Sizes Women's Medium, Women's Large/Men's Small, Men's Medium, and Men's Large Only:

RND 6: Knit.

RND 7: [K2tog, k– (–, –, 0) (1, 2, 2)] twice, k2tog, knit to end— – (–, –, 4) (6, 8, 8) sts remain.

Sizes Men's Medium and Men's Large Only:

RND 8: Knit.

RND 9: [K2tog, k1] twice, k2tog—5 sts remain.

All Sizes:

Cut yarn, leaving a long tail. Thread tail through remaining sts, pull tight, and fasten off.

FINISHING

Using tail, close gap at base of thumb. Fold cuff lining to WS and loosely tack in place, being careful not to let sts show on RS.

Block as desired.

KNIT PUMPKINS

....

Autumn seems to be the time of year when people start to return indoors, and in anticipation of the upcoming holidays, the urge to decorate the house arises. These pumpkins are a joy to knit—and you can use just about any type of yarn in any gauge. Make a bunch of them and give a friend a selection for their home, or display them on a festive dinner table or on top of the hearth.

SIZES
Small (Medium, Large)

FINISHED MEASUREMENTS
Circumference
Small: 12" (30.5 cm) circumference x 2" (5 cm) tall
Medium: 14½" (37 cm) circumference x 2¼" (5.5 cm) tall
Large: 20¼" (51.5 cm) circumference x 3½" (9 cm) tall

YARN
Small: Patons Classic Wool Worsted [100% pure new wool; 210 yards (192 meters) / 100 grams]: 1 skein Pumpkin (A)
Medium: Blue Sky Fibers Printed Organic Cotton [100% certified organic cotton; 150 yards (137 meters) / 100 grams]: 1 hank #2200 Jack Frost (B)
Large: Lion Brand Wool-Ease Thick & Quick [80% acrylic, 20% wool; 106 yards (97 meters) / 6 ounces (171 grams)]: 1 skein #135 Spice (C)
Miscellaneous yarn scraps for stems and tendrils in green and brown

NEEDLES
Small: Needle(s) in preferred style for small-circumference knitting in the rnd, size US 6 (4 mm)

Medium: Needle(s) in preferred style for small-circumference knitting in the rnd, size US 7 (4.5 mm)

Large: Needle(s) in preferred style for small-circumference knitting in the rnd, size US 11 (8 mm)

NOTIONS

Stitch marker, polyester fiberfill or repurposed stuffing

GAUGES

24 sts and 28 rnds = 4" (10 cm) in St st, using A and size US 6 (4 mm) needle(s)

18 sts and 22 rnds = 4" (10 cm) in St st, using B and size US 7 (4.5 mm) needle(s)

10 sts and 14 rnds = 4" (10 cm) in St st, using C and size US 11 (8 mm) needle(s)

PATTERN NOTE

This pattern will work with any yarn. When choosing needles, select a needle size smaller than what the ball band suggests so that the fabric is tightly knit. This will ensure that the stuffing will not show through. Feel free to experiment by casting on more stitches for a larger pumpkin and adding rounds to change the size.

PUMPKIN

With yarn of your choice and matching size needle(s), CO 34 sts, leaving at least an 8" (40.5 cm) tail. Join for working in the rnd, being careful not to twist sts; pm for beginning of rnd. Knit 1 rnd.

SHAPE BOTTOM

INCREASE RND: *K1, k1-f/b; repeat from * to end—51 sts.
Work 24 rnds in St st (knit every rnd).

SHAPE TOP

DECREASE RND: *K1, k2tog; repeat from * to end—34 sts remain.
Knit 1 rnd. Cut yarn, leaving a 1½ yard (1.5 m) tail. Thread tail through remaining sts and pull to close. Bring yarn through to WS and close up hole further. Move needle over half a st, then bring yarn back up through center top to the RS.
Thread CO tail through sts of Increase Rnd and pull to close slightly, leaving a hole for stuffing. Stuff to desired stiffness (a tighter fill shows more detail) and close hole tightly, then sew a few stitches to secure. Tie a knot and run the needle through the pumpkin and out one side,

then trim end close to surface of pumpkin. Use this same technique later to hide ends after attaching stems and tendrils.

RIDGES

Thread tail at top of pumpkin through tapestry needle; take needle through center of top and out center of bottom. Bring needle up along one side of pumpkin, through top center, then out bottom center again, and pull tight to create a ridge. Continue to add ridges in this fashion until you like the way it looks. When ridges are complete, take yarn through to the bottom and secure.

STEM

Using scrap yarn of your choice and needle(s) appropriate to that yarn, work a 5 (5, 8)-st I-cord (see Special Techniques, page 168) to desired length. BO all sts, then thread tail through BO sts to close up. Using CO tail, attach I-cord to top of pumpkin.

TENDRILS

Using scrap yarn of your choice and needle(s) 2–3 sizes larger than needle size appropriate to that yarn, CO sts equaling roughly the length of desired coiled tendril.

NEXT ROW: *K1-f/b/f; repeat from * to end.

BO all sts. Coax tendril into a coil and attach to top of pumpkin using tail.

PURLED PUMPKIN

To make the purled version shown, which has taller proportions, work an additional 8 rnds before shaping top. Turn pumpkin inside out (leaving tails to purl side) before closing and stuffing.

CRAZY CONED CAP

....

What can I say? We all have relatives or friends who'd rock a crazy cap like this. If it's a bit much, select just one or two colors, cast on, and go!

SIZES
To fit sizes youth–adult
NOTE: Size may be adjusted by adding or subtracting increases; see Pattern Notes and instructions.

FINISHED MEASUREMENTS
20" (50 cm) circumference at brim

YARN
Koigu Painters Palette Premium Merino (KPPPM) [100% merino wool; 170 yards (155 meters) / 50 grams]: 1 skein each #P517 (orange) (A), #P536 (green) (B), #P108 (coral) (C), and #P135 (burgundy) (D)

NEEDLES
One 16" (40 cm) long circular needle size US 3 (3.25 mm)

Needle(s) in preferred style for small-circumference knitting in the rnd, size US 3 (3.25 mm) Change needle size if necessary to obtain correct gauge.

NOTIONS
Stitch markers (including one in unique color or style for beginning of rnd), removable stitch marker, tassel maker or pom-pom maker

GAUGE
28 sts and 40 rnds = 4" (10 cm) in St st

STITCH PATTERNS

STRIPE SEQUENCE
Work *A, B, C, D; repeat from * to end.

1X1 RIB

(even number of sts; 1-rnd repeat)

ALL RNDS: *K1, p1; repeat from * to end.

PATTERN NOTE

This cap is worked from the top down.

To adjust the final circumference, work more or fewer increase rounds. Every increase round added or subtracted will change the circumference by 1" (2.5 cm).

HAT

Using needle(s) in preferred style for small-circumference knitting in the rnd and A, CO 14 sts. Join for working in the rnd, being careful not to twist sts; pm in unique color or style for beginning of rnd.

RND 1: Knit.

RND 2: *K1, k1-f/b, pm; repeat from * to end, omitting final pm (beginning-of-rnd marker is here)—21 sts.

RNDS 3–11: Knit.

RND 12 (INCREASE RND): *K1-f/b, knit to marker, sm; repeat from * to end—7 sts increased.

RND 13: Change to B; knit.

RND 14: Change to A; knit. Cut A and continue with B.

RNDS 15–21: Knit.

RND 22 (INCREASE RND): Repeat Rnd 12—35 sts.

RND 23: Change to C; knit.

RND 24: Change to B; knit. Cut B and continue with C.

RNDS 25–31: Knit.

RND 32 (INCREASE RND): Repeat Rnd 12—42 sts.

RND 33: Change to D; knit.

RND 34: Change to C; knit. Cut C and continue with D.

RNDS 35 AND 36: Knit.

RND 37 (INCREASE RND): Repeat Rnd 12—49 sts.

RNDS 38–41: Knit.

RND 42 (INCREASE RND): Repeat Rnd 12—56 sts.

NOTE: Change to circular needle if necessary for number of sts on needle(s).

Repeat Rnds 33–42 six more times (or to desired circumference), changing to next color in Stripe Sequence on every repeat of Rnd 33, working Rnd 34 with old color, then returning on Rnd 35 to new color; increase 7 sts every repeat of Rnds 37 and 42—140 sts. Place removable marker on first st of rnd.

Work even, continuing color changes every 10 rnds as established, until piece measures approximately 6½" (16.5 cm) from removable marker, or to 1" (2.5 cm) less than desired length, ending with final rnd of stripe, and removing all markers except beginning-of-rnd marker on final rnd. **NOTE:** If necessary, decrease 1 st on final rnd so you have an even number of sts.

Change to your preferred color (sample used C) and 1x1 Rib; work even for 1" (2.5 cm).

BO all sts in pattern.

FINISHING

Make a tassel (see Special Techniques, page 171) or pom-pom with the same color as the ribbing and attach to top of hat.

DIAGONAL STRIPED THROW BLANKET

Here's a simple diagonal blanket that you can make any size you want. It's easy to follow the directions because they are a recipe, more or less. If you have a set quantity of yarn, grab a kitchen scale and keep track of how much yarn you're using. You will want to use roughly half of it before "turning the corner" and finishing the second half of the blanket.

BABY BLANKET	**36" × 36"** (91.5 × 91.5 cm)
LAPGHAN	36" × 48" (91.5 × 122M)
FULL-SIZE THROW BLANKET	**48" × 48-60"** (122 × 122-152.5 cm)

GETTING STARTED

Knit a gauge swatch in Garter stitch (knit all rows) and write down the number of stitches you get per inch or centimeter and make note of your goal width. Multiply your goal width by the number of stitches per inch or centimeter you have in your swatch. That will be the number of stitches you will start out with. After that, continue to knit in rows and follow the Diagonal Knit Blanket pattern, but instead continue increasing until the piece is as wide as you want it to be. From there, begin to work straight (on right sides, K2, M1, work to last 4 sts, k2; on the wrong side, work as before).

Continue in this manner—working on the straight portion of your blanket—until you again want to turn the corner or make the bottom edge of your blanket. When you have reached this point, you will again follow the pattern and on right sides you will k2, ssk, work to the last 2 sts, then knit to end; on wrong sides, work as established. Once you have just 5 stitches remaining on your blanket, bind off.

You can use the same technique for making a diagonally knit throw blanket in just about any size. Here are a few typical sizes for throw blankets.

FINISHED MEASUREMENTS

Approximately 37" (94 cm) wide x 53" (134.5 cm) long

YARN

Scheepjes Stone Washed XL [70% cotton, 30% acrylic; 82 yards (75 meters) / 50 grams]: 3 skeins each #843 Black Onyx (A), #854 Crystal Quartz (B), #872 Enstatite (C), #841 Moon Stone (D), #873 Beryl (E), and #870 Lepidolite (F)

NEEDLES

One 32" (80 cm) long or longer circular needle size US 8 (5 mm) Change needle size if necessary to obtain correct gauge.

NOTIONS

Kitchen scale

GAUGE

19 sts and 24 rows = 4" in Garter st (knit every row)

STITCH PATTERN

COLOR SEQUENCE

Work *A, B, C, D, E, then F; repeat from * through end of blanket.

PATTERN NOTE

Circular needle is used to accommodate the larger number of stitches; do not join.

This pattern is very flexible. You can make a blanket with one, two, three, or more colors as long as you start out with the same amount of yarn in the same weight.

Because skein weights can vary, it is essential to know the weight of each color you have in order to avoid running out of yarn. Before you begin, weigh all three skeins of each color together and note the weight; you should have close to 150 grams in each color. Note the lightest weight of three skeins in one color. The blanket will be worked based on half of the lightest weight; it should be roughly 75 grams after being divided in half.

You may adjust the length and width of the blanket; instructions for adjustment are included in the pattern. If you increase the size of the blanket, you may need to purchase additional yarn.

BLANKET

Using A, CO 5 sts.

SET-UP ROW 1 (WS): P2, knit to last 2 sts, p2.

ROW 1 (RS): K2, M1L, knit to last 2 sts, M1L, k2—2 sts increased.

ROW 2: P2, knit to last 2 sts, p2.
Repeat Rows 1 and 2, changing to the next color in Color Sequence after using just short of one half of the total three-skein weight of the previous color (in this case, roughly 75 grams; see Pattern Notes). Continue until piece measures approximately 37" (94 cm) or your desired blanket width along one edge, ending with a WS row.

ROW 3 (RS): K2, M1R, knit to last 4 sts, k2tog, k2.

ROW 4: P2, knit to last 2 sts, p2.
Continuing in Color Sequence, repeat Rows 3 and 4 until piece measures approximately 53" (94 cm) or to desired total length along longer side edge, ending with a WS row.

ROW 5 (RS): K2, ssk, knit to last 4 sts, k2tog, k2—2 sts decreased.

ROW 6: P2, knit to last 2 sts, p2.
Continuing in Color Sequence, repeat Rows 5 and 6 until 7 sts remain, ending with a WS row.

NEXT ROW (RS): K1, ssk, k1, k2tog, k1—5 sts remain.
Bind off all sts knitwise.

FINISHING

Block as desired.

Winter

If you are a knitter, winter has to be the season when you most want to knit but have the least amount of time in which to do it! There are just so many activities: decorating our homes, baking cookies and cakes, sending holiday cards, planning last-minute gifts, and attending or throwing parties. The air smells of pine and fireplaces, of cinnamon and spiced tea. This is the time when we want to wear and give the warmest sweaters, the fluffiest socks, the coziest mittens, and the most festive holiday-themed household items.

"Winter is not a season, it's a celebration." —ANAMIKA MISHRA

"When it snows you have two choices: shovel or make snow angels." —ANONYMOUS

"I wonder if the snow loves the trees and fields, that it kisses them so gently? And then it covers them up snug, you know, with a white quilt; and perhaps it says, 'Go to sleep, darlings, till the summer comes again.'" —LEWIS CARROLL

"Winter is the time for comfort, for good food and warmth, for the touch of a friendly hand and for a talk beside the fire: it is the time for home." —EDITH SITWELL

"Snow was falling, / so much like stars filling the dark trees / that one could easily imagine / its reason for being was nothing more / than prettiness." —MARY OLIVER

CABLED TABLE RUNNER

I always envision a table runner like this on a rustic farm table, or on a mantel over a fireplace. This is one of those items that someone will keep forever and pull out every winter to cozy things up. Take a look at the table below for common table lengths—table runners are pretty flexible when it comes to length. They can hang over the ends of the table or lie on top.

FINISHED MEASUREMENTS
14" (35.5 cm) wide x 56" (142 cm) long

YARN
Spud & Chloë Outer [65% superwash wool, 35% certified organic cotton; 60 yards (55 meters) / 100 grams]: 5 skeins #7216 Snow Day

NEEDLES
One pair straight needles size US 13 (9 mm)
Change needle size if necessary to obtain correct gauge.

NOTIONS
Cable needle, stitch markers

GAUGE
14 sts and 11 rows = 4" (10 cm) in St st

SPECIAL ABBREVIATIONS
C8B: Slip 4 sts to cable needle, hold to back, k4, k4 from cable needle.
C8F: Slip 4 sts to cable needle, hold to front, k4, k4 from cable needle.

TABLE RUNNER LENGTHS

With tables, there are plenty of standard sizes. If you're looking to outfit a particular table and want to veer from the pattern, you will have to decide if you want the runner to stay on the table while there are plates on it and people are eating, or if you want it to be decorative and sit with the ends of the runner hanging over the edges. I tend to let it be whatever it wants to be, but you may be different.

Usually, a place setting will take about 12" (30.5 cm) of vertical space. So, if you want the table runner to stay on the table while eating, you will want to subtract that amount of space from each side of the table (assuming it is rectangular) before you decide what width and length you want your runner. If you are a visual person, just draw the table with its dimensions, then draw in the table runner, plot out how you want it to be oriented on the table, and take it from there. Circular tables, on the other hand, don't really have too many rules, although it makes more sense to knit a runner that is shorter than the diameter of the table, because if the runner edges fall over the curved edge, it may not look nice and neat.

Take the following common table sizes into account while you knit the Cabled Table Runner so you can make it as long as you want it to be.

WIDTH	LENGTH	SEATING
2'6"	3'6"	2
2'6"	5'0"	4–6
3'0"	6'0"	6–8
3'6"	8'0"	8–10
4'6"	10'0"	10–12

STITCH PATTERN

PLAITED CABLE

NOTE: You may work Plaited Cable from text or chart.
(panel of 12 sts; 12-row repeat)
ROW 1 (RS): Knit.
ROW 2 AND ALL WS ROWS: Purl.
ROW 3: C8F, k4.
ROWS 5 AND 7: Knit.
ROW 9: K4, C8B.
ROW 11: Knit.
ROW 12: Purl.
Repeat Rows 1–12 for Plaited Cable.

TABLE RUNNER

CO 36 sts.
SET-UP ROW (WS): K2, pm, k10, pm, k12, pm, k10, pm, k2.
ROW 1 (RS): K2, sm, p10, sm, work Plaited Cable to marker, sm, p10, sm, k2.
ROW 2: K2, sm, k10, sm, work Plaited Cable to marker, sm, k10, sm, k2.

Work even until piece measures 56" (142 cm) from the beginning, ending with Row 6 or 12 of pattern.
BO all sts in pattern.

FINISHING
Block as desired.

Plaited Cable

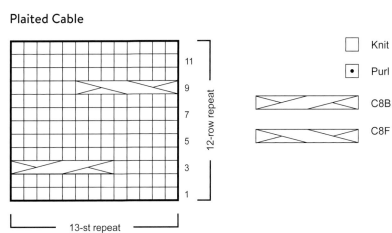

	Knit
⊡	Purl

C8B

C8F

SLOUCHY BED SOCKS

No matter the climate, there's always a warm and cozy factor we savor when it is holiday time. These slouchy socks are quickly knit with larger-gauge yarn that is brushed and fluffy, so they are extra comfy. Size up for an even slouchier fit.

SIZES

Children's Large/Women's Small (Women's Medium/Men's Small, Women's Large/Men's Medium, Men's Large)

FINISHED MEASUREMENTS

8 (9¼, 10¾, 12)" [20.5 (23.5, 27.5, 30.5) cm] foot circumference
NOTE: These socks are intended to be slightly loose fitting.

YARN

Buttercream Luxe Craft Angel Hair [50% acrylic, 28% nylon, 22% wool; 120 yards (110 meters) / 100 grams): 1 (2, 2, 2) skeins Pale Pink

NEEDLES

One set of four or five double-pointed needles size US 10 (6 mm)
Change needle size if necessary to obtain correct gauge.

NOTIONS

Stitch marker

GAUGE

12 sts and 18 rnds = 4" (10 cm) in Thermal Stitch

STITCH PATTERNS

2X2 RIB

(multiple of 4 sts; 1-rnd repeat)
ALL RNDS: *K2, p2; repeat from * to end.

THERMAL STITCH

(multiple of 4 sts; 4-rnd rep)

RNDS 1 AND 2: Knit.

RNDS 3 AND 4: *K2, p2; repeat from * to end.

Repeat Rnds 1–4 for Thermal Stitch.

PATTERN NOTES

These socks are worked from the cuff down, with double-wrapped short rows to shape the heels.

CUFF

CO 24 (28, 32, 36) sts. Divide sts evenly among 3 or 4 needles, with half of the sts on the first 2 needles for the instep and the remainder on 1 or 2 needle(s) for the heel. Join for working in the rnd, being careful not to twist sts; pm for beginning of rnd.

Begin 2x2 Rib; work even for 1½" (4 cm).

LEG

Begin Thermal Stitch; work even until piece measures approximately 5 (6, 6½, 7)" [12.5 (15, 16.5, 18) cm] from the beginning, ending with Rnd 4 of pattern.

SHORT-ROW HEEL

PARTIAL RND: Knit to end of instep; leave instep sts out of work on two needles. Work on 12 (14, 16, 18) heel sts only, working all heel sts onto one needle if necessary.

SHORT ROW 1 (RS): K11 (13, 15, 17) w&t.

SHORT ROW 2 (WS): P10 (12, 14, 16) w&t.

SHORT ROW 3: Knit to 1 st before wrapped st from previous RS row, w&t.

SHORT ROW 4: Purl to 1 st before wrapped st from previous WS row, w&t.

Repeat Short Rows 3 and 4 two (3, 3, 4) more times—4 (4, 6, 6) sts remain between wrapped sts at center of heel.

NOTE: In the following short rows, you may either work the wraps together with their wrapped sts as you come to them or leave the wraps in place, as was done for the socks shown.

SHORT ROW 5 (RS): Knit to first wrapped st from previous RS row, knit wrapped st, w&t.

SHORT ROW 6 (WS): Purl to first wrapped st from previous WS row, purl wrapped st, w&t.

SHORT ROW 7: Knit to double-wrapped st from previous RS row, w&t.

SHORT ROW 8: Purl to double-wrapped st from previous WS row, w&t.

Repeat Short Rows 7 and 8 until all wrapped sts have been worked. On last repeat of Short Rows 7 and 8, you will work the final w&t of each row on the first st on either side of the heel sts.

PARTIAL RND: Knit to end of heel sts.

FOOT

Work even in St st (knit every rnd) until piece measures 8¼ (8¾, 9¾, 9½)" [21 (22, 25, 24) cm] from back of heel, or to 1½ (2, 2, 2½)" [4 (5, 5, 6.5) cm] less than desired foot length.

TOE

DECREASE RND: K1, ssk, knit to last 3 instep sts, k2tog, k1, sm, k1, ssk, knit to last 3 heel sts, k2tog, k1—4 sts decreased.

Repeat Decrease Rnd every other rnd 3 (4, 4, 5) more times—8 (8, 12, 12) sts remain.

Knit 1 rnd.

Cut yarn, leaving a 10" (25.5 cm) tail. Arrange sts onto 2 needles and graft toe sts using Kitchener st (see Special Techniques, page 169).

FINISHING

Block as desired.

SAMPLER CAP

....

Looking for a gift that has just the right number of elements to keep it interesting to knit? Try out this pattern. It can be made in a multitude of colors, and it just begs for customization. You can follow the pattern, make stripes, or even knit it solid instead. The pom-pom is optional, and if you're not sure if your recipient will like the pom-pom, just attach it as you usually would, and tie a bow to the wrong side with your yarn ends so they can remove it. (This is a good trick regardless, so that it can be removed for laundering.)

SIZES
Toddler/Child (Adult Medium, Adult Large)

FINISHED MEASUREMENTS
18 (20, 22)" [45.5 (51, 56) cm] circumference

YARN
Blue Sky Fibers Baby Alpaca [100% baby alpaca; 110 yards (100 meters) / 50 grams]: 2 skeins #505 Natural Taupe (MC); 1 skein each #522 Denim (A), #508 Natural Medium Gray (B), and #806 Salsa (C)

NEEDLES
One 16" (40 cm) long circular needle size US 3 (3.25 mm) Needle(s) in preferred style for small-circumference knitting in the rnd, size US 3 (3.25 mm) Change needle size if necessary to obtain correct gauge.

NOTIONS
Stitch markers (including one in unique color or style for beginning of rnd); 1⅝" (45 mm) pom-pom maker

GAUGE

24 sts and 32 rows = 4" (10 cm) in St st

STITCH PATTERN

1X1 RIB

(even number of sts; 1-rnd repeat)

ALL RNDS: *K1, p1; repeat from * to end.

PATTERN NOTE

When changing colors for stripes, if distance to next instance of old color is shorter than 1" (2.5 cm), carry color not in use up inside of hat; otherwise, cut yarn and rejoin again when needed.

HAT

Using MC and needle(s) in preferred style for small-circumference knitting in the rnd, CO 108 (120, 132) sts. Join for working in the rnd, being careful not to twist sts; pm in a unique color or style for beginning of rnd.

Begin 1x1 Rib; work even for 1" (2.5 cm).

Change to A and St st (knit every rnd); work 5 (4, 4) rnds even.

Work Rnds 1 and 2 of Chart A.

Change to A; knit 5 rnds.

Change to MC; knit 2 (3, 3) rnds.

Work Rnds 1–5 of Chart B.

Change to MC; knit 2 (3, 3) rnds.

Change to A; knit 2 rnds.

Change to MC; knit 1 rnd.

Work Rnds 1–3 of Chart C.

Change to MC; knit 1 rnd.

Change to A; knit 2 rnds.

Change to MC; knit 3 (3, 3) rnds.

Change to B; knit 1 rnd.

Work Rnds 1–4 of Chart D.

Change to B; knit 1 rnd.

Change to MC.

Size Toddler/Child Only:

NEXT RND: [K25, k2tog] 4 times—104 sts remain.

Sizes Adult Medium and Adult Large Only:

Knit 3 rnds.

Work Rnds 1–6 of Chart E.

Size Adult Large Only:

NEXT RND: [K31, k2tog] 4 times—128 sts remain.

All Sizes:

Knit 1 rnd, pm every 13 (15, 16) sts (omit last pm; beginning-of-rnd marker is here).

SHAPE CROWN

NOTE: Change to needle(s) in preferred style for small-circumference knitting in the rnd when necessary for number of sts on needle.

DECREASE RND: *Knit to 3 sts before marker, ssk, k1, sm; repeat from * to end—8 sts decreased.

Repeat Decrease Rnd every other rnd 11 (12, 13) more times—8 (16, 16) sts remain; 1 (2, 2) st(s) remain(s) between markers.

Knit 1 rnd, removing markers.

Cut yarn, leaving a long tail.

Thread tail through remaining sts, pull tight, and fasten off.

FINISHING

Using pom-pom maker, make pom-pom using primarily MC, adding other colors in as desired. Attach pom-pom to top of hat. Block as desired.

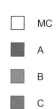

MC

A

B

C

Chart A

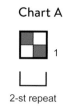

1

2-st repeat

Chart B

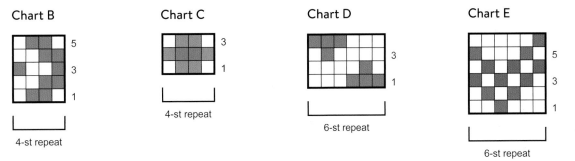

5

3

1

4-st repeat

Chart C

3

1

4-st repeat

Chart D

3

1

6-st repeat

Chart E

5

3

1

6-st repeat

STUFFED MITTENS

Living in Southern California most of my life, I guess I don't know or remember what really cold weather feels like—but I do remember being little in Minnesota and playing in the snow. I have seen mittens like these here and there, and they look so warm and comfy, I just had to make them. They're filled with *thrums*, multicolored tufts of wool roving. Making thrums is addictive, and picking out colors for your creation will be lots of fun. Note: The thrums do take up a lot of room inside the mitten, so size up if you're not sure about the fit.

SIZES

6–9 years (10 years–Women's X-Small, Women's Medium, Unisex Large)

FINISHED MEASUREMENTS

7 (8, 9, 10, 11)" [18 (20.5, 23, 25.5, 28) cm] hand circumference

YARN

Morehouse Farm 3-Strand Worsted Weight Yarn [100% merino wool; 145 yards (132 meters) / 2 ounces (57 grams)]:

1 (1, 2, 2, 2) skein(s) Sky (MC) EcoSoft Wool Roving [100% wool; 1 ounce (28 grams)]: 1 ounce each Cotton Candy, Rhubarb, and Natural

NEEDLES

One set of four or five double-pointed needles size US 7 (4.5 mm)
One set of four or five double-pointed needles size US 8 (5 mm)
Change needle size if necessary to obtain correct gauge.

NOTIONS

Stitch markers, waste yarn

GAUGE

16 sts and 20 rnds = 4" (10 cm) in St st

STITCH ABBREVIATION

Thrum 1: Insert needle into st below next st on left needle, wrap thrum over right needle, pull thrum through st, k1-tbl into st above thrum (first st on left needle), pass thrum over last st on right needle, tug back of thrum gently into place.

STITCH PATTERNS

TWISTED RIB

(even number of sts; 1-rnd repeat)
ALL RNDS: *K1-tbl, p1; repeat from * to end.

THRUM PATTERN

(multiple of 4 sts; 5-rnd repeat)
NOTE: Change roving colors randomly.
RND 1: *K3, thrum 1; repeat from * to end.
RNDS 2–4: Knit.
RND 5: K1, thrum 1, *k3, thrum 1; repeat from * to last 2 sts, k2. Repeat Rnds 1–5 for Thrum Pattern.

PATTERN NOTES

Start out by making lots and lots of thrums. You will be surprised how many you will use. Take a look at the tutorial before starting. Your thrums should begin with about 5–6" (12.5–15 cm) of roving, with slightly thick centers and ends that are feathery. Fold each thrum in half with the two ends meeting in the middle and twist the centers together.

CUFF

Using smaller needles, CO 24 (28, 32, 36, 40) sts. Join for working in the rnd, being careful not to twist sts; pm for beginning of rnd.
Begin Twisted Rib; work even until piece measures 2¾ (3, 3, 3, 3¼)" [7 (7.5, 7.5, 7.5, 8.5) cm] from the beginning.

HAND

Change to larger needles and St st (knit every rnd); knit 1 rnd.
NEXT RND: K3 (3, 4, 4, 5), [M1L, k6 (7, 8, 9, 10)] 3 times, M1L, k3 (4, 4, 5, 5)—28 (32, 36, 40, 44) sts.
Begin Thrum Pattern; work even until piece measures 3 (3½, 4, 4½, 5)" [7.5 (9, 10, 11.5, 12.5) cm] from end of ribbing.

PLACE THUMB

NEXT RND: Using waste yarn, work 8 sts, transfer these 8 sts back to left needle, change to working yarn, work to end.

Work even until piece measures 6½ (7, 7½, 8, 8½)" [16.5 (18, 19, 20.5, 21.5) cm] from end of ribbing, placing marker after 14 (16, 18, 20, 22) sts on final rnd.

SHAPE TOP

DECREASE RND: [K1, ssk, work to 3 sts before marker, k2tog, k1, sm] twice—4 sts decreased.

Repeat Decrease Rnd every other rnd 3 (3, 3, 3, 4) more times—12 (16, 20, 24, 24) sts remain. Divide sts onto 2 needles and graft sts using Kitchener st (see Special Techniques, page 169).

THUMB

Remove waste yarn and place live thumb sts onto 2 dpns, with half on top needle and half on bottom needle.

NEXT RND: Rejoin yarn. With first needle, pick up and knit 1 st in corner of thumb, knit across bottom sts; with second needle, pick up and knit 1 st in corner of thumb, k4; with third needle, k4—18 sts.

NEXT RND: Needle 1: K2tog, knit to end of needle; Needle 2: K2tog, knit to end of needle; Needle 3: Knit to end—16 sts remain.

Begin Thrum Pattern; work even until piece measures 2 (2, 2½, 3, 3)" [5 (5, 6.5, 7.5, 7.5) cm].

DECREASE RND: *K1, k2tog; repeat from * to last st, k1—11 sts remain. Knit 1 rnd.

DECREASE RND: *K2tog; repeat from * to last st, k1—6 sts remain. Break yarns, leaving a 6" (15 cm) long tail; thread tail through remaining sts, pull tight, and fasten off.

FINISHING

Soak with wool wash in lukewarm or cool water without agitating. Squeeze out water and lay flat to dry. If necessary, turn inside out to dry completely (and enjoy the beautiful sight).

MAKING THRUMS

Have your roving ready to go.
Pull a 4–5" (10–13 cm) long
section off the roving. It should
be narrow—about a quarter inch
(6 mm) wide. Lay the roving
on a flat surface. Using your
fingers, tug slightly on each
end to lengthen the piece into
a thin strip, then wrap it around
two fingers to make a loop and
twist it to make a figure eight.
Roll the center of the thrum
between your forefinger and
thumb to tack it together and
make a flat section of about ⅓"
(8 mm) long between the two
looped ends.

AFTERTHOUGHT THUMBS

There is more than one way to knit thumbs into mittens. The Family of Striped Mittens on page 109 feature gussets. These are triangular sections of extra fabric you add while you are knitting the body of the mitten, and later those added stitches are separated and made into a thumb. The Stuffed Mittens here, on the other hand, feature what I call afterthought thumbs, because they are literally added last. Whenever you knit a mitten pattern, you have a choice: You can knit a gusset if the pattern tells you to, or you could instead make afterthought thumbs (as long as there isn't special patterning on the gusset). All you have to do is follow the guidelines here and omit the gusset instructions in your mitten pattern. As an aside, these guidelines assume that you have some access to another mitten that fits the recipient or know how their hand is shaped and its size.

1. Knit your mitten in the round as directed until the knitting reaches the base of the thumb. Work to the end of the round or to the needle that holds the stitches for the back of the hand, cut the working yarn, and work about 1½" (4 cm) worth of stitches in a contrasting color of waste yarn. (You can also skip breaking the yarn and instead work the stitches in your contrasting yarn, slip them back onto the left-hand needle, then work across the same stitches again with the working yarn. This way, you will have fewer ends of yarn to weave in.)

2. Complete the mittens as directed.

3. Pick out the waste yarn to expose the thumb stitches, and place the bottom and top live stitches onto three double-pointed needles.

4. Join the working yarn and work across the first needle, then pick up and knit one or two stitches from the gap between the top and the bottom stitches. Continue across the needle, holding the top stitches, and when you get to the second gap, pick up and knit the same number of stitches as you did before.

5. Place a marker and join to work in rounds. Work even until the thumb tube just reaches the end of the thumb.

6. To shape the thumb, *k2tog; repeat from * to the end, working k3tog at the end if you have an odd number of stitches on the needles. Break the yarn and draw the tail through the remaining live stitches, bring the yarn to the inside, and fasten off.

HOLIDAY TREE SKIRT

One year I received a Christmas tree skirt as a hostess gift. I didn't quite know what to make of it, because it was unexpected and an unusual gift. After twenty years, I still use that skirt, and I fondly remember the person who gave it to me. Since then, I have given items like this as gifts—and they are always well received and a huge surprise. Although this skirt is a bit kitschy and funky, I quite like it, and it will make a great gift for that youthful someone you know who loves a pop of color and fun. To make it smaller, either use a smaller-gauge yarn or stop knitting when it is the size you want it to be.

FINISHED MEASUREMENT
Approximately 20" (51 cm) length from inside edge to bound-off edge

YARN
Skirt: Lion Brand Yarn Side Dish [100% cotton; 46 yards (42 meters) / 100 grams]; 12 skeins #100 White (MC).
NOTE: Nearly all of the 12th skein was used for the sample. Due to variations in knitter gauge, you may wish to purchase an additional skein to ensure you don't run out.

Pom-Poms: Brown Sheep Company Nature Spun Sport [100% wool; 184 yards (168 meters) / 1¾ ounces (50 grams)]: 1 skein each #720 Ash, #105 Bougainvillea, #112 Elf Green, #108 Cherry Delight, and #N78 Turquoise Wonder. **NOTE:** Each pom-pom weighs an average of 4 grams; there are 23 pom-poms on the skirt. The same colors were used for the Peppermint Candy Coasters on page 165.

NEEDLES
One 40" (100 cm) long or longer circular needle size US 15 (10 mm) Change needle size if necessary to obtain correct gauge.

NOTIONS
1½" (4 cm) pom-pom maker, sturdy thread or button thread

GAUGE
8 sts and 12 rnds = 4" (10 cm) in St st

STITCH PATTERN

RIDGE PATTERN
(any number of sts)
ROW 1: Knit.
ROW 2: Purl.
ROWS 3 AND 4: Knit.
Repeat Rows 1–4 for Ridge Pattern.

PATTERN NOTES
This tree skirt is worked from the center out. You may adjust the size of the skirt by using a different size needle, by adding or subtracting stitches at the cast-on edge, or by working more or fewer increase rows.
The number of stitches doubles with every increase row; the number of rows from one increase row to the next doubles as well.

SKIRT
Using MC, CO 24 sts.
Knit 1 row, purl 1 row.
INCREASE ROW (RS): *K1-f/b; repeat from * to end—48 sts.
Knit 1 row.
Begin Ridge Pattern; work 6 rows even.
Continue in Ridge Pattern for remainder of skirt.
Repeat Increase Row—96 sts.
Work 11 rows even.
Repeat Increase Row—192 sts.
Work 23 rows even.
Repeat Increase Row—384 sts.
Work even until piece measures 20" (51 cm) from the beginning, ending with a RS row.
NOTE: You may work a larger tree skirt if desired by working another Increase Row a total of 48 rows from the previous Increase Row.
BO all sts knitwise on WS.

FINISHING
Block as desired.
Make four or five 1½" (4 cm) pom-poms in each color. Use strong thread or button thread to tie off pom-poms, leaving a long enough tail to attach pom-poms to edges approximately 7–7½" (18–19 cm) apart around circumference of skirt.

FELT BALL WREATH

A wreath hanging on your door or over a window is the quintessential winter holiday decoration. This snowball wreath is fun to make and something anyone would want to bring out year after year to celebrate the season. If you desire, you can make a smaller version and gift it as a base for a pillar candle—just find a wreath base that is smaller in circumference.

FINISHED MEASUREMENT
Approximately 12" (30.5 cm) diameter circle

MATERIALS
Weir Crafts Undyed NZ Corriedale Wool Roving (100% wool): approximately 16 ounces (457 grams) Natural Off-White
NOTE: You may also use wool-blend roving.
Several yards (meters) of worsted-weight wool or wool-blend yarn in similar color to wrap wreath form

NOTIONS
9–10" (23–25.4 cm) Styrofoam wreath form, glue gun and glue sticks, wide ribbon for hanging

FELT BALLS
NOTE: Follow instructions on page 151 for making felt balls. Make felt balls in a range of sizes, from approximately ¾" to 1½" (19 to 38 mm). The sample used approximately 200 balls, but depending upon the size of the wreath form used and the size of the felt balls, yours may take more or fewer; begin with 50 balls and see how they fit on your wreath form, then make more until the wreath is filled in as desired.

Imagine all the different things you can make with felt balls: You can follow the same principle as the Snowball Wreath and, using a smaller form, make a candle base. You can string the felt balls to make a garland like the one on page 105 or string them closer together and make a disk (glue together using a glue gun) that can be used as a coaster, a trivet, or a wall hanging.

If you love to knit, chances are you've come upon wool roving—wool that has been cleaned and combed but not yet spun into yarn. Wool roving doesn't have to be turned into yarn, it can be made into felted figures, pretty pin cushions, it can be stuffed into pillows and made into felt balls for cats to play with or used as ornaments or in craft projects.

Making felt balls is a super fun crafting project that can be used for all manner of decorative items like garlands, wreaths, and felt-ball flower bouquets. They can be strung and formed into, say a trivet, or even planets that hang and create a solar system.

If you want to make felt balls, you'll need real wool, or at least a blend of fiber that has a significant amount of wool in it. Craft stores usually carry wool for felting that has an amount of man-made fiber, but that's okay. If you desire, you can order pure wool for felting by the ounce or the pound from online sources (see page 174 for the supplier I use).

HOW TO MAKE FELT BALLS

Before getting started. Heat some water in a kettle and get a big bowl. Fill half with cool water, add a teaspoon or so of dish soap, and then add hot water. The water will need to be hot, but not so hot that it burns your hands. Place your fiber on the table next to the bowl.

1. Pull off a bit of fiber. Depending upon they type of wool you have, you'll either rip a bit off or you'll have to pull the fiber (hairs) away from the roving. Stretch out the fiber so it's not in one clump and separate the hairs or the fiber. Form a round wad a little less than an inch.

2. Take more wool and spread it out and wrap it around the original wad. Don't smoosh it together. Keep things kind of loose and neat. You don't want to your felt ball to have cracks in it.

1

Continue to add layers of fiber until the ball is at least twice the size you want it to be. (If you are planning on making a lot of same-size balls, you can use a sensitive scale to weigh them.)

2

3. Submerge the ball of wool into the soap solution and hold it in there and feel the water saturate the ball. Do not squeeze it.

4. Carefully remove the ball and hold it in your palm. Slowly coax it into a sphere as the water runs out.

3

5. Hold the ball between your palms and roll the ball in a circular motion. Continue to do this (it's okay to change directions) without applying too mush pressure. As you do this, you will notice the ball beginning to firm up.

6. Examine your felt ball. If there are cracks, dry your hands and remove a small amount of fiber from your dry roving and lay it over the crack and drape it nicely over your ball. Place it gently back into the water and feel the water saturate it. Remove it from the water again and roll the ball in your hands.

4

7. If your water is very soapy, run the felt ball under cool water (do not squeeze) and allow the ball to air dry.

5

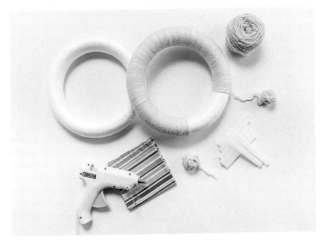

FINISHING

After all the felt balls are dry, and using a similar color of worsted-weight yarn and a glue gun, wrap the wreath form. Only a couple of dots of glue on the front and the back are necessary to hold the yarn in place.

After the wreath form is wrapped, begin to attach one ball at a time on the form using a small amount of glue for each ball. Work your way around the form and attach felt balls as you like. Reserve the smallest balls to fill cracks, and be sure to apply the largest ones sparingly and evenly around the form.

Once dry, choose a ribbon and hang the wreath from it as shown.

PARIS IN WINTER BERET

. . . .

Berets make great gifts, especially for that one friend or family member who's very fashion-forward. This project takes only one ball of yarn, is a quick knit, and can be worn a multitude of ways.

SIZES
18 months–4 years (5 years–Adult Small, Adult Medium, Adult Large)

FINISHED MEASUREMENTS
16 (17, 18¼, 19)" [40.5 (43, 46.5, 48.5) cm] circumference at brim, slightly stretched

YARN
Valley Yarns Wachusett [70% merino wool / 30% cashmere; 163 yards (149 meters) / 50 grams]: 1 ball

NEEDLES
One 16" (40 cm) long circular needle size US 7 (4.5 mm)
One set of double-pointed needles size US 7 (4.5 mm)
Change needle size if necessary to obtain correct gauge.

NOTIONS
Stitch markers in two colors

GAUGE
18 sts and 24 rnds = 4" (10cm) in St st

STITCH PATTERN

1X1 RIB
(even number of sts; 1-rnd repeat)
ALL RNDS: *K1, p1; repeat from * to end.

HAT
Using circular needle, CO 72 (76, 82, 86) sts. Join for working in the rnd, being careful not to twist sts; pm in a unique color for beginning of rnd.
Work in St st (knit every rnd) for 4 (6, 6, 6) rnds.
Change to 1x1 Rib; work 3 rnds even.

BODY
INCREASE RND: *K2, M1L; repeat from * to end—108 (114, 123, 129) sts.
Work even until piece measures 3 (3¾, 4½, 5)" [7.5 (9.5, 11.5, 12.5) cm] from beginning of ribbing.
Sizes Adult Medium and Adult Large Only:
NEXT RND: [K- (-, 39, 41), k2tog] 3 times— - (-, 120, 126) sts remain.
All Sizes:
NEXT RND: Knit, placing markers every 18 (19, 20, 21) sts.

CROWN
NOTE: Change to dpns when necessary for number of sts on needle.
DECREASE RND: *Knit to 2 sts before marker, k2tog, sm; repeat from * to end—6 sts decreased.
Repeat Decrease Rnd every rnd 16 (17, 18, 19) more times, removing all but beginning-of-rnd marker on final rnd—6 sts remain.
NEXT RND: *K2tog; repeat from * to end—3 sts remain.
Transfer remaining sts to one dpn and work 3-st I-Cord (see Special Techniques, page 168) for approximately ¾ (1, 1, 1)" [2 (2.5, 2.5, 2.5) cm].
BO all sts.
Cut yarn, leaving a 6" (15 cm) tail.

FINISHING
Thread I-Cord tail onto tapestry needle, fold I-Cord in half and take needle through base of I-Cord to WS, secure tail, and weave in end.
Block beret as desired, using a small plate inside damp beret to set the shape.

HOLIDAY LIGHTS SWEATER

....

This round-yoke sweater pattern is sized to make pullovers for the whole family. Built from the bottom up and knit in the round, this sweater is a great gift that can be customized for any color palette you like. You'll want to knit it again and again for your family, your friends, even yourself.

SIZES

To fit: youth 22–23 (24–25, 26–27, 28–29, 30–31) [adult 32–33 (34–35, 36–37, 38–39) (40–41, 42–43, 44–45) (46–47, 48–49, 50–51)]" / 56–58.5 (61–63.5, 66–68.5, 71–73.5, 76–78.5) [81.5–84 (86.5–89, 91.5–94, 96.5–99) (101.5–104, 106.5–109, 112–114.5) (117–119.5, 122–124.5, 127–129.5)] cm chest

NOTE: Sweater is intended to be worn with approximately 3–4" (7.5–10 cm) ease. Youth sizes are presented first, with adult sizes in brackets. If there is only one number before or within the brackets, all sizes in that range are worked the same for that instruction.

FINISHED MEASUREMENTS

25½ (28, 29½, 32, 34½) [36 (37½, 40, 42½) (44, 46½, 48) (50½, 52, 54½)]" / 65 (71, 75, 81.5, 87.5) [91.5 (95.5, 101.5, 108) (112, 118, 122) (128.5, 132, 138.5)] cm chest circumference

YARN

Cascade Yarns Cascade 220 [100% Peruvian highland wool; 220 yards (200 meters) / 100 grams]: 2 (3, 3, 3, 4) [4 (5, 5, 6) (6, 6, 7) (7, 7, 8)] hanks #8393 Dark Navy (MC); 1 hank each #8010 Natural (A), #2413 Red (B), and #9451 Lake Chelan Heather (C)

NEEDLES

One 24 [32]" / 60 [80] cm long circular needle size US 7 (4.5 mm) Needle(s) in preferred style for small-circumference knitting in the rnd, size US 7 (4.5 mm) Change needle size if necessary to obtain correct gauge.

NOTIONS

Stitch markers (including one in unique color or style for beginning of rnd), waste yarn

GAUGE

20 sts and 24 rnds = 4" (10 cm) in St st

STITCH PATTERN

1X1 RIB
(even number of sts; 1-rnd repeat)
ALL RNDS: *K1, p1; repeat from * to end.

PATTERN NOTES

This sweater is worked in the round from the bottom up. The body is worked first, then set aside while the sleeves are worked. The pieces are then joined, and the yoke is worked in the round to the top with short-row shaping to shape the back neck.

BODY

Using circular needle and MC, CO 128 (140, 148, 160, 172) [180 (188, 200, 212) (220, 232, 240) (252, 260, 272)] sts. Join for working in the rnd, being careful not to twist sts; pm for beginning of rnd. Begin 1x1 Rib; work even for 1½" (4 cm).
Change to St st (knit every rnd); work even until piece measures 8½ (9½, 11, 12½, 14) [14 (14, 14½, 15¼) (16, 16¼, 16½) (16¾, 17, 17¼)]" / 21.5 (24, 28, 32, 35.5) [35.5 (35.5, 37, 38.5) (40.5, 41.5, 42) (42.5, 43, 44)] cm from the beginning, ending 4 [5 (5, 5, 5) (5, 7, 7) (7, 7, 7)] sts before beginning of rnd.

DIVIDE FOR FRONT AND BACK

DIVISION RND: BO 8 [10 (10, 10, 10) (10, 14, 14) (14, 14, 14)] sts (removing marker), k56 (62, 66, 72, 78) [80 (84, 90, 96) (100, 102, 106) (112, 116, 122)] sts (including st on right needle after BO), BO the next 8 [10 (10, 10, 10) (10, 14, 14) (14, 14, 14)] sts, knit to end—56 (62, 66, 72, 78) [80 (84, 90, 96) (100, 102, 106) (112, 116, 122)] sts remain each for front and back. Cut yarn and set aside, leaving sts on needle.

SLEEVES

Using needle(s) in preferred style for small-circumference knitting in the rnd, CO 30 (32, 36, 38, 40) [46 (46, 50, 50) (50, 54, 54) (54, 58, 58)] sts. Join for working in the rnd, being careful not to twist sts; pm for beginning of rnd. Begin 1x1 Rib; work even for 1½ [2]" / 4 [5] cm. Change to St st; work 5 [6] rnds even.

SHAPE SLEEVE

INCREASE RND: K1-f/b, work to last st, k1-f/b, k1—2 sts increased. Repeat Increase Rnd every 6 (6, 8, 6, 6) [8 (8, 8, 6) (6, 6, 6) (6, 6, 4)] rnds 6 (9, 8, 2, 2) [4 (8, 6, 2) (4, 2, 9) (16, 12, 1)] more time(s), then every 8 (0, 0, 8, 8) [10 (10, 10, 8) (8, 8, 8) (8, 8, 6)] rnds 2 (0, 0, 7, 8) [5 (2, 4, 10) (9, 11, 6) (1, 4, 17)] time(s)—48 (52, 54, 58, 62) [56 (58, 62, 66) (68, 68, 72) (76, 78, 82)] sts.
Work even until piece measures 11½ (12, 13½, 14¼, 15½) [16¾ (17¼, 17¾, 18½) (19, 19¾, 20¼) (20½, 20½, 20¾)]" / 29 (30.5, 34.5, 36, 39.5) [42.5 (44, 45, 47) (48.5, 50, 51.5) (52, 52, 52.5)] cm from the beginning, ending 4 [5 (5, 5, 5) (5, 7, 7) (7, 7, 7)] sts before beginning of rnd; BO the next 8 [10 (10, 10, 10) (10, 14, 14) (14, 14,

14)] sts (removing marker)—40 (44, 46, 50, 54) [66 (68, 72, 76) (78, 82, 86) (90, 92, 96)] sts remain. Cut yarn, transfer sts to waste yarn, and set aside. Repeat for second sleeve, leaving sts on needle(s). Do not cut yarn.

YOKE

JOINING RND: With RS facing, using circular needle and yarn attached to second (left) sleeve, knit across 40 (44, 46, 50, 54) [56 (58, 62, 66) (68, 68, 72) (76, 78, 82)] left sleeve sts, pm, knit across 56 (62, 66, 72, 78) [80 (84, 90, 96) (100, 102, 106) (112, 116, 122)] front sts, pm, knit across 40 (44, 46, 50, 54) [56 (58, 62, 66) (68, 68, 72) (76, 78, 82)] right sleeve sts, pm, knit across 56 (62, 66, 72, 78) [80 (84, 90, 96) (100, 102, 106) (112, 116, 122)] back sts, place unique marker for beginning of rnd—192 (212, 224, 244, 264) [272 (284, 304, 324) (336, 340, 356) (376, 388, 408)] sts.

NEXT RND: Knit, decreasing a total of 2 (2, 4, 4, 4) [2 (4, 4, 4) (1, 0, 1) (1, 3, 3)] st(s) evenly spaced, working the decrease(s) right before or after sleeve marker(s)—190 (210, 220, 240, 260) [270 (280, 300, 320) (335, 340, 355) (375, 385, 405)] sts remain.

Work even until piece measures 1½ (1¾, 2, 2, 2) [2 (2¼, 2¼, 2½) (2½, 2½, 2½) (2½, 2¾, 2¾)]" / 4 (4.5, 5, 5, 5) [5 (5.5, 5.5, 6.5) (6.5, 6.5, 6.5) (6.5, 7, 7)] cm from Joining Rnd.

SHAPE YOKE AND WORK CHART

NOTES: Chart and yoke shaping are worked at the same time; please read entire section through before beginning. In the charts, each simple 2-rnd colorwork section is followed by 2 plain St st rnds in A. Work each Decrease Rnd on the second of these plain St st rnds. When working decreases across a marker, replace the marker after working the decrease.

DECREASE RND 1: *K3, k2tog; repeat from * to end—152 (168, 176, 192, 208) [216 (224, 240, 256) (268, 272, 284) (300, 308, 324)] sts remain.

Begin Chart A – Youth [Chart B – Adult]; continuing to work Decrease Rnds as follows, work to end of chart once, then change to MC and work in MC for remainder of Yoke.

Continuing to work chart as established, work even until piece

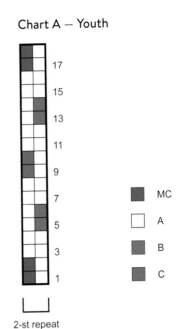

Chart A — Youth

17
15
13
11
9
7
5
3
1

MC
A
B
C

2-st repeat

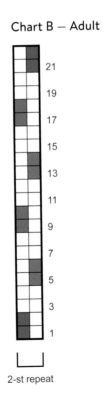

Chart B — Adult

21
19
17
15
13
11
9
7
5
3
1

2-st repeat

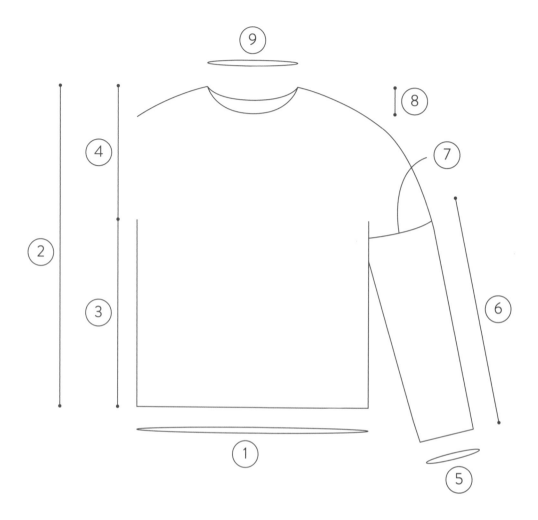

1   25½ (28, 29½, 32, 34½) [36 (37½, 40, 42½) (44, 46½, 48) (50½, 52, 54½)]"
       65 (71, 75, 81.5, 87.5) [91.5 (95.5, 101.5, 108) (112, 118, 122) (128.5, 132, 138.5)] cm

2   15½ (17½, 19½, 21½, 23½) [24 (24½, 25½, 26½) (27½ 27¾, 28¼) (28¾, 29¼, 29¾)]"
       39.5 (44.5, 49.5, 54.5, 59.5) [61 (62, 65, 67.5) (70, 70.5, 72) (73, 74.5, 75.5)] cm

3   8½ (9½, 11, 12½, 14) [14 (14, 14½, 15¼) (16, 16¼, 16½) (16¾, 17, 17¼)]"
       21.5 (24, 28, 32, 35.5) [35.5 (35.5, 37, 38.5) (40.5, 41.5, 42) (42.5, 43, 44)] cm

4   7 (8, 8½, 9, 9½) [10 (10½, 11, 11¼) (11½, 11½, 11¾) (12, 12¼, 12½)]"
       18 (20.5, 21.5, 23, 24) [25.5 (26.5, 28, 28.5) (29, 29, 30) (30.5, 31, 32)] cm

5   6 (6½, 7¼, 7½, 8) [9¼ (9¼, 10, 10) (10, 10¾, 10¾) (10¾, 11½, 11½)]"
       15 (16.5, 18.5, 19, 20.5) [23.5 (23.5, 25.5, 25.5) (25.5, 27.5, 27.5) (27.5, 29, 29)] cm

measures approximately 2¾ (3¼, 3¾, 4, 4) [4 (4½, 4½, 4¾) (5, 5, 5) (5, 5¼, 5½)]" / 7 (8.5, 9.5, 10, 10) [10 (11.5, 11.5, 12) (12.5, 12.5, 12.5) (12.5, 13.5, 14)] cm from Joining Rnd, ending with the nearest first plain St st rnd in A in the chart.

DECREASE RND 2: *K2, k2tog; repeat from * to end—114 (126, 132, 144, 156) [162 (168, 180, 192) (201, 204, 213) (225, 231, 243)] sts remain.

Work even until piece measures approximately 4 (4¼, 5¼, 5¾, 6) [6 (6½, 6¾, 7) (7¼, 7¼, 7½) (7½, 7¾, 8)]" / 10 (11, 13.5, 14.5, 15) [15 (16.5, 17, 18) (18.5, 18.5, 19) (19, 19.5, 20.5)] cm from Joining Rnd, ending with the nearest first plain St st rnd in A in the chart.

DECREASE RND 3: *K1, k2tog; repeat from * to end—76 (84, 88, 96, 104) [108 (112, 120, 128) (134, 136, 142) (150, 154, 162)] sts remain.

Work even until piece measures approximately 5¼ (6¼, 6¾, 7¼, 7¾) [8 (8¾, 9, 9¼) (9¾, 9¾, 9¾) (10, 10¼, 10¾)]" / 13.5 (16, 17, 18.5, 19.5) [20.5 (21.5, 23, 23.5) (24, 24, 25) (25.5, 26, 26.5)] cm from Joining Rnd. You should have completed the chart.

SHAPE NECK

NOTE: Neck is shaped using short rows (see Special Techniques, page 171).

SHORT ROW 1 (RS): Knit to marker, sm, w&t, sm.

SHORT ROW 2 (WS): Purl to third marker, sm, w&t, sm.

SHORT ROW 3: Knit to 6 sts before wrapped st from previous RS row, w&t.

SHORT ROW 4: Purl to 6 sts before wrapped st from previous WS row, w&t.

SHORT ROW 5: Knit to end.

Knit 1 rnd, working wraps together with wrapped sts as you come to them.

DECREASE RND 4: *K1, k2tog; repeat from * to last 1 (0, 1, 0, 2) [0 (1, 0, 2) (2, 1, 1) (0, 1, 0)] st(s), [k2tog] 0 (0, 0, 0, 1) [0 (0, 0, 1) (1, 0, 0) (0, 0, 0)] time(s), k1 (0, 1, 0, 0) [0 (1, 0, 0) (0, 1, 1) (0, 1, 0)]—51 (56, 59, 64, 69) [72 (75, 80, 85) (89, 91, 95) (100, 103, 108)] sts remain. Knit 1 rnd, decreasing 1 (0, 1, 0, 1) [0 (1, 0, 1) (1, 1, 1) (0, 1, 0)] st(s)— 50 (56, 58, 64, 68) [72 (74, 80, 84) (88, 90, 94) (100, 102, 108)] sts remain. Change to 1x1 Rib; work even for ¾ [1]" / 2 [2.5] cm. BO all sts loosely.

FINISHING

Using tails, sew underarm sts. Block as desired.

6   11½ (12, 13½, 14¼, 15½) [16¾ (17¼, 17¾, 18½) (19, 19¾, 20¼) (20½, 20½, 20¾)]"
29 (30.5, 34.5, 36, 39.5) [42.5 (44, 45, 47) (48.5, 50, 51.5) (52, 52, 52.5)] cm

7   9½ (10½, 10¾, 11½, 12½) [13¼ (13½, 14½, 15¼) (15½, 16½, 17¼) (18, 18½, 19¼)]"
24 (26.5, 27.5, 29, 32) [33.5 (34.5, 37, 38.5) (39.5, 42, 44) (45.5, 47, 49)] cm

8   1"
2.5 cm

9   10 (11¼, 11½, 12¾, 13½) [14½ (14¾, 16, 16¾) (17½, 18, 18¾) (20, 20½, 21½)]"
25.5 (28.5, 29, 32.5, 34.5) [37 (37.5, 40.5, 42.5) (44, 45.5, 47.5) (51, 52, 54.5)] cm

PEPPERMINT CANDY COASTERS

....

These coasters are great take-along projects that can be knit up while waiting for whatever you wait for or to bring to occasions where you can fit in some stitches here and there. Choose any color combo for just about any occasion. If you knit these in pure wool, over time they will felt a bit and become a sturdy and memorable heirloom that will be brought out every year or used year-round. Add or subtract stitches when you cast on for smaller-sized discs as decorations or larger-sized ones that can become washcloths.

FINISHED MEASUREMENTS
Approximately 4¾" (12 cm) diameter

YARN
Brown Sheep Company Nature Spun Sport [100% wool; 184 yards (168 meters) / 1¾ ounces (50 grams)]: 1 skein each #720 Ash (MC), #105 Bougainvillea (CC), #112 Elf Green (CC), #108 Cherry Delight (CC), and #N78 Turquoise Wonder (CC)
NOTE: One skein of MC will yield approximately 6 coasters.

NEEDLES
One pair straight needles size US 5 (3.75 mm)
Change needle size if necessary to obtain correct gauge.

GAUGE
22 sts and 32 rows (16 ridges) = 4" (10 cm) in Garter st (knit every row)
NOTE: Gauge is not essential for this project.

PATTERN NOTES

These coasters are worked flat; the wedges are shaped using short rows (see Special Techniques, page 171). There is no need to hide the wraps while knitting the coaster; they will not be noticeable in the Garter st fabric.

All color changes occur in the center of the coaster; do not cut yarn when changing colors.

All short rows are worked with the WS facing.

You may work a smaller or larger coaster; see instructions for how to adjust the size. Adjusting the size will affect the amount of yarn required for each coaster.

COASTER

With CC of choice, CO 14 sts.

NOTE: To work a smaller or larger coaster, CO fewer or more sts in multiples of 2.

WEDGE 1

ROW 1 (WS): Knit to last 4 sts, w&t.

ROW 2: Knit.

ROW 3: Knit to 2 sts before wrapped st from previous WS row, w&t.

ROW 4: Knit.

ROWS 5–10: Repeat Rows 3 and 4 four times. **NOTE:** If you adjusted the CO st count, repeat Rows 3 and 4 until you have worked k2, w&t on the final repeat of Row 3; end with a Row 4.

ROW 11: Knit.

ROW 12: Change to next color. Knit.

WEDGE 2–11

Work as for Wedge 1.

NOTE: If you adjusted the number of CO sts, determine the number of wedges to work by subtracting 2 from your CO st count. This number is the total number of wedges to work. Work your final wedge as for Wedge 12, as follows:

WEDGE 12

Work Rows 1–9 of Wedge 1.

NOTE: If you adjusted the number of CO sts, work until you have worked k2, w&t on the final repeat of Row 3, ending with a Row 3.

BO all sts; cut yarn, leaving a tail approximately 3 times the width of the BO edge.

FINISHING

With RS facing, using tail from BO row, sew BO edge to CO edge. Thread tail through sts around center hole, pull tight to close, and fasten off.

Soak coasters in lukewarm water and wool wash. Block as desired.

SPECIAL TECHNIQUES

Backward Loop CO: Make a loop (using a slipknot) with the working yarn and place it on the right-hand needle (first st CO), *wind yarn around thumb clockwise, insert right-hand needle into the front of the loop on thumb, remove thumb and tighten st on needle; repeat from * for remaining sts to be CO, or for casting on at the end of a row in progress.

When working the CO at the end of a row, *wind yarn around thumb clockwise, insert right-hand needle into the front of the loop on the thumb, remove thumb, and tighten st on needle; repeat from * for remaining sts needed. When working the CO at the beginning of a row, work as above, inserting left-hand needle instead of right-

hand needle into the loop on the thumb.

If you are someone who relies on the Backward Loop method, by all means, expand your horizons if you're willing to! The next step I'd suggest is to give the Long-Tail Cast-On a try. It is the one I almost always use and is featured in nearly every pattern in this book. It's only slightly trickier than Backward Loop, and chances are, if you know other knitters or have access to the internet, you can ask for a demonstration or seek out a video. The great thing about the long-tail version is that it creates an elastic edge, it looks nice, and it works well for pretty much any stitch pattern and any type of project.

Crab Stitch: Work the same as for Single Crochet, but work in the opposite direction.

Crochet Chain: Holding tail end of yarn in left hand, *take hook under ball end of yarn from front to back; draw yarn on hook back through previous st on hook to form new st. Repeat from * to desired number of sts or length of chain.

I-Cord: Using a double-pointed needle, cast on or pick up the required number of sts; the working yarn will be at the left-hand side of the needle. *Transfer the needle with the sts to your left hand, bring the yarn around behind the work to the right-hand side; using a second double-pointed needle, knit the sts from right to left, pulling the yarn from left to right for the first st; do not turn. Slide the sts to the opposite end of the needle; repeat from * until the I-Cord is the length desired. Note: After a few rows, the tubular shape will become apparent.

Kitchener Stitch: Using a blunt tapestry needle, thread a length of yarn approximately 4 times the length of the section to be joined. Hold the pieces wrong sides together, with the needles holding the sts parallel, both ends pointing to the right. Working from right to left, insert tapestry needle into first st on front needle as if to purl, pull yarn through, leaving st on needle; insert tapestry needle into first st on back needle as if to knit, pull

yarn through, leaving st on needle; *insert tapestry needle into first st on front needle as if to knit, pull yarn through, remove st from needle; insert tapestry needle into next st on front needle as if to purl, pull yarn through, leave st on needle; insert tapestry needle into first st on back needle as if to purl, pull yarn through, remove st from needle; insert tapestry needle into next st on back needle as if to knit, pull yarn through, leave st on needle. Repeat from *, working 3 or 4 sts at a time, then go back and adjust tension to match the pieces being joined. When 1 st remains on each needle, cut yarn and pass through last 2 sts to fasten off.

Long-Tail CO: Leaving a tail with about 1" (2.5 cm) of yarn for each st to be CO, make a slipknot in the yarn and place it on the right-hand needle, with the tail end in the front and the working end in the back. Insert the thumb and forefinger of your left hand between the strands of yarn so that the working end is around your forefinger and the tail end is around your thumb in a slingshot fashion; *insert the tip of the right-hand needle into the front loop on the thumb, hook the strand of yarn coming from the forefinger from back to front, and draw it through the loop on your thumb; remove your thumb from the loop and pull on the working yarn to tighten the new st on the right-hand needle; return your thumb and forefinger to their original positions, and rep from * for remaining sts as needed. There are a few patterns that begin with a ribbed edging like the Holiday Lights Sweater on page 159 and the Tassel Tank on page 81. Although I've used the Long-Tail Cast-On most in this book, there are times when I want a nice, stretchy, neat and clean edge, and for that I used a stretchy cast-on. There are five or six varieties that I've read about, but the one that I find reliable is the Alternating Long-Tail Cast-On. It's a variation of the Long-Tail Cast-On many of us know, and it works especially well with projects that start out with ribbing and ask for a pretty edge. What's nice about this cast-on is that as you place your stitches on the needles, you can create any pattern of ribbing to match your project. For example, if you're starting with a k2, p2 rib for a neck edging in a top-down pattern, you can cast on in that pattern. One thing to be aware of is that some people need to go up a needle size when they are casting on, so whatever you do, give it a try with the yarn you're planning to use for a trial run before you commit.

Alternating Long-Tail CO: This cast-on alternates a traditional long-tail cast-on with a reversed long-tail cast-on that looks like a purl stitch. Set up just as you would for a long-tail cast-on. The tail is on the left over the thumb as with the regular CO; when you want to mimic a knit st, the needle travels behind and through the thumb loop from left to right, then across to pluck the yarn over the finger and bring it back through the thumb loop. To make what looks like a purl stitch, the needle travels to the outside of the finger loop, through the loop from right to left, then over to the thumb yarn. Grab the thumb yarn from beneath and bring it through the finger loop. Scoot the yarn up to the needle, but not too tightly. Alternatively, you will want to avoid casting on too loosely, because the structure of the rib you are creating will be lost. You can combine knit and purl cast-on stitches to match any type of rib you'd like.

Placing Live Stitches on Waste Yarn: Thread a tapestry needle with a length of yarn that will hold the piece you are working on. Using the tip of the needle, slide each live stitch off of the knitting needle and onto the waste yarn.

Provisional Cast-On: Using crochet hook and waste yarn, work a crochet chain with a few more chains than the number of sts needed; fasten off. If desired, tie a knot on the fastened-off end to mark the end that you will be unraveling from later. Turn the chain over; with working yarn, starting a few chains in from the beginning of the chain, pick up and knit one st in each bump at the back of the chain, leaving any extra chains at the end unworked.

When ready to work the live sts, unravel the chain by loosening the fastened-off end and unzipping the chain, placing the live sts on a spare needle.

Short Row Shaping: Work the number of sts specified in the instructions, wrap and turn (w&t) as follows:

To wrap a knit st, bring yarn to the front (purl position), slip the next st purlwise to the right-hand needle, bring yarn to the back of work, return the slipped st on the right-hand needle to the left-hand needle purlwise; turn, ready to work the next row, leaving the remaining sts unworked. To wrap a purl st, work as for wrapping a knit st, but bring yarn to the back (knit position) before slipping the st, and to the front after slipping the st. When short rows are completed, or when working progressively longer short rows, work the wrap together with the wrapped st as you come to it as follows:

If st is to be worked as a knit st, insert the right-hand needle into the wrap, from below, then into the wrapped st; k2tog. If st to be worked is a purl st, insert needle into the wrapped st, then down into the wrap; p2tog. (Wrap may be lifted onto the left-hand needle, then worked together with the wrapped st if this is easier.)

Single Crochet: Make a slipknot and place on hook. *Insert hook into next st (along lower or upper edge) or between two rows (side edges). Yo hook, pull through to RS—2 loops on hook. Yo hook, draw through both loops—1 loop on hook. Repeat from * to end.

Slip Stitch: Insert your hook into the next stitch, Yarn Over, pull it out of your stitch AND through the loop you have on your hook.

Tassels: Wind yarn 20 times (or to desired thickness) around a piece of cardboard or other object the same length as desired for tassel. Slide tapestry needle threaded with matching yarn under the strands at the top of the tassel; tie tightly, leaving ends long enough for attaching tassel to garment. Cut through all strands at the opposite end. Tie a second piece of yarn tightly around the tassel several times, approximately ½" (1.5 cm) from top of tassel; secure ends inside top of tassel. Trim ends evenly; attach to garment.

Three-Needle Bind-Off:
Place the sts to be joined onto two same-size needles (or two ends of a circular needle); hold the pieces to be joined with the right sides facing each other and the needles parallel, both pointing to the right. Holding both needles in your left hand, using working yarn and a third needle same size or one size larger, insert third needle into first st on front needle, then into first st on back needle; knit these two sts together; *knit next st from each needle together (two sts on right-hand needle); pass first st over second st to BO one st. Repeat from * until one st remains on third needle; cut yarn and fasten off.

ABBREVIATIONS

BO – Bind off

CC – Contrast color

CO – Cast on

Dpn – Double-pointed needle(s)

K1-f/b – Knit into the front loop and back loop of the same stitch to increase 1 stitch.

K1-f/b/f – Knit into the front loop, back loop, and front loop of the same stitch to increase 2 stitches.

K1-tbl – Knit 1 stitch through the back loop.

K2tog – Knit 2 stitches together.

K – Knit

M1L (make 1 left slanting) – With the tip of the left-hand needle inserted from front to back, lift the strand between the 2 needles onto the left-hand needle; knit the strand through the back loop to increase 1 stitch.

M1R (make 1 right slanting) – With the tip of the left-hand needle inserted from back to front, lift the strand between the 2 needles onto the left-hand needle; knit the strand through the front loop to increase 1 stitch.

Mb – Make bobble (as instructed).

MC – Main Color

P1-f/b – Purl into the front loop and back loop of the same stitch to increase 1 stitch.

P2tog – Purl 2 stitches together.

Pm – Place marker

P – Purl

Rnd(s) – Round(s)

RS – Right side

Sk2p (double decrease) – Slip the next stitch knitwise to the right-hand needle, k2tog, pass the slipped stitch over the stitch from the k2tog.

Sm – Slip marker

Sp2p (double decrease) – Slip the next stitch purlwise to the right-hand needle, p2tog, pass the slipped stitch over the stitch from the p2tog.

Ssk (slip, slip, knit) – Slip the next 2 stitches to the right-hand needle one at a time as if to knit; return them to the left-hand needle one at a time in their new orientation; knit them together through the back loops.

Ssp (slip, slip, purl) – Slip the next 2 stitches to the right-hand needle one at a time as if to knit; return them to the left-hand needle one at a time in their new orientation; purl them together through the back loops.

St(s) – Stitch(es)

WS – Wrong side

W&t – Wrap and turn (see Special Techniques—Short Row Shaping)

Wyib – With yarn in back

Wyif – With yarn in front

YARN SOURCES AND SUPPLIES

Bartlett Yarns
Harmony, ME
Bartlettyarns.com

Bernat
Listowel, Ontario, Canada
yarnspirations.com/
    our-brands/bernat

Berroco
North Smithfield, RI
Berroco.com

**Blue Sky Fibers / Spud
    & Chloë**
Minneapolis, MN
Blueskyfibers.com

Brown Sheep Company
Mitchell, NE
Brownsheep.com

Cascade Yarns
Seattle, WA
Cascadeyarns.com

Ewe Ewe Yarns
Oceanside, CA
Eweewe.com

**Juniper Moon Farm/
Knitting Fever**
Central VA
Knittingfever.com

Lion Brand Yarn
Carlstadt, NJ and New
    York, NY
Lionbrand.com

Koigu
Chatsworth, Ontario
Koigu.com

Morehouse Farm
Red Hook, New York
Morehousefarm.com

Patons
West Yorkshire, United
    Kingdom
Knitpatons.com

Premier Yarns
Harrisburg, NC
Premieryarns.com

Rowan Yarns
Wakefield, West Yorkshire,
    United Kingdom
Knitrowan.com

Scheepjes
Tynaarlo, The Netherlands
Scheepjes.com

Valley Yarns
Northampton, MA
Yarn.com

Weir Crafts (EcoSoft Roving)
Milan, OH
Weircrafts.com

ACKNOWLEDGMENTS

Today, as I prepared to write this, I thought of the first person I ever knit for. He was a boy I met in school when I was about seventeen. I had picked up the needles again after being taught a long time before and decided I would knit him a present for Christmas.

I went to the local craft store and picked up yarn in a variety of colors and weights—I didn't know at the time that mixing yarns in various weights didn't always work in one's favor. I didn't know, either, that when you knit a scarf, you needed to add in a non-rolling edge. My urge to make him a scarf right then and there was so powerful, I didn't take even one moment to consider any of this.

So, I cast on as my grandmother taught me (backward loop) and knit one side and purled the other side and changed colors here and there. As I knit, I thought of him and how excited he would be when he opened his handmade gift. I knit until I ran out of yarn and bound off what had become a twenty-foot-long scarf.

The moment I took that thing off the needles it turned into a wild snake. It rolled up on itself and no matter what I did to tame it, it just rolled and rolled and rolled. I looked at it and worried about whether I should give it to him. What if he didn't like it? What if he laughed? What if…?

This is what we go through as knitters: We learn the craft and the very first thing that comes to mind is knitting a gift for someone we love. We hear of a baby coming and what do we do? We knit booties! We see the seasons change to cooler weather and what do we do? We knit a sweater! Looks like snow? Make socks! Buds on the tree branches? Make a scarf!

I'm so happy to have made this book of gifts for all seasons, but without the help of my editor, Meredith Clark, and tech editor, Sue McCain, it would not have been possible. Their combined expertise helped keep me grounded so I could write and design without worrying about every little detail. Thanks to you both. Also thanks go out to Darilyn Lowe Carnes for the artistic details in the layout and to Carla Choy for the photographs and styling. Lastly, thank you to my husband, Theron Tan, for the action shots and for standing by me every, single moment.

And just so you know: that young man for whom I made that epically rolled scarf? He loved it.

Editor: Meredith A. Clark
Designer: Darilyn Lowe Carnes
Production Manager: Kathleen Gaffney

Library of Congress Control Number: 2021932511

ISBN: 978-1-4197-4624-6
eISBN: 978-1-68335-956-2

Printed and bound in China
10 9 8 7 6 5 4 3 2 1

Abrams books are available at special discounts when purchased in quantity
for premiums and promotions as well as fundraising or educational use.
Special editions can also be created to specification. For details, contact
specialsales@abramsbooks.com or the address below.

Abrams® is a registered trademark of Harry N. Abrams, Inc.

ABRAMS The Art of Books
195 Broadway, New York, NY 10007
abramsbooks.com